I0448233

As of May 17, 2012, this guidance applies to federal savings associations in addition to national banks.*

AM-IMS

Comptroller of the Currency
Administrator of National Banks

Investment Management Services

Comptroller's Handbook

August 2001

AM

Asset Management

Investment Management Services   Table of Contents

Introduction

For purposes of this booklet, investment management is defined as the business of managing or providing advice on investment portfolios or individual assets for compensation. Investment management is one of the financial service industry's primary product offerings and generates considerable revenue. National banks are significant providers of investment management services, and for many it is a key strategic line of business.

This booklet contains an overview of the investment management business, its associated risks, and an appropriate risk management framework. It provides national bank examiners with supervisory guidance for examining and monitoring these activities in large banks and, if applicable, community banks. Also included in the booklet is supervisory guidance for assessing and monitoring risks associated with functionally regulated activities. The "References" section of this booklet provides sources of information on portfolio management, including Web-based financial glossaries. The glossaries define the investment concepts and terms used in this booklet, and the other resources provide in-depth information on the booklet's topics.

This booklet applies to accounts administered by national banks acting in a fiduciary capacity and holding discretionary investment powers. It also applies to nondiscretionary accounts for which a national bank is an investment adviser if the bank receives a fee for its investment advice. "Fiduciary capacity," "investment discretion," and "investment adviser" are defined in 12 CFR 9.2 and 9.101, Fiduciary Activities of National Banks.

Background

Investment management is a very competitive business with many different types of service providers. Increasing numbers of financial and nonfinancial companies now declare savings and investment products and services to be their core competence. A number of factors have made investment management one of the fastest growing and competitive businesses in the financial services industry. These factors include tremendous growth in assets under management, the globalization of capital markets, the proliferation of investment alternatives, changes in client demographics and relationships, and rapid technological advancements.

The attraction to this business is profitability. In some segments of the investment management business, pretax operating margins often surpass 25 percent. Institutional retirement and investment company accounts are typically the most profitable. The personal wealth management business generates somewhat lower, but still attractive, pretax operating margins. This line of business requires a higher level of personalized service, and the accounts are usually smaller than on the institutional side. Personal wealth management is also one of the fastest growing segments of the industry.

The primary challenge for service providers has been to keep pace with changes in the industry. Investments have taken on new forms in response to changes in investor characteristics and demands, financial regulation, political environments, and technological abilities. While investors and their portfolio managers, or advisers, still concentrate on traditional investments vehicles, such as publicly traded stocks and bonds, an increasing number of investment alternatives, such as real estate, hedge funds, and other unregistered private investments, are used as a means of enhancing a portfolio's risk-return relationships.

The investment management industry is in transition, and though it offers the opportunity for significant, recurring fee income, effectively managing the business's risks poses tremendous challenges.

Portfolio Management and Advisory Services

National banks provide investment management services to clients with differing characteristics, investment needs, and risk tolerance. A bank is usually paid a percentage of the dollar amount of assets being managed in the client's portfolio. If an account's total assets are below a minimum, it often pays a fixed fee. Other factors in the amount of fees are an account's complexity and other banking relationships. Some banks have advisory agreements that base compensation on performance. In this type of arrangement, the portfolio manager, or adviser, receives a percentage of the return achieved over a given time period.

National banks manage and provide advice on all types of assets for their clients. Besides managing portfolios of publicly traded stocks and bonds, national banks also manage and provide advice for portfolios that include a broad range of investment alternatives such as financial derivatives, hedge funds, real estate, private equity and debt securities, mineral interests, and art. Refer to the *Comptroller's Handbook for Fiduciary Activities* for information on individual investment categories and related risk management processes.

Investment management services are provided in two primary types of accounts: separately managed accounts and commingled or pooled investment funds. Two types of pooled investment funds are collective investment funds and mutual funds. A fiduciary portfolio manager may invest a separately managed account's assets in these types of funds to help achieve its investment goals and objectives.

Separately Managed Accounts

A separately managed account is created solely for the purpose of investing a client's funds on a stand-alone basis. There are two primary types of accounts for which a national bank provides investment management services: trusts and investment agency accounts. National banks may also be responsible for separately managed accounts when serving as an executor, administrator, guardian, or in any other fiduciary capacity.

Trusts

National banks have long served as trustees with investment authority for private trusts. Private trusts are established or created for the benefit of a designated individual or individuals, or a known person or class of persons, identified by the terms of the instrument creating the trust. Trusts are generally created through a trust instrument established during the life of the grantor, through a will at the time of a testator's death, or through a court order.

The investment authority and duties of a trustee are derived from the trust instrument (to the extent the trust's terms are possible and legal) and through other applicable law. A trustee may have sole or shared investment authority or discretion. The trust instrument may restrict a trustee's investment options as well as prohibit the trustee from selling certain trust assets.

Investment Agency Accounts

Agency accounts are governed by the terms of the contract establishing the relationship, by state law, and by common agency and contract law principles. A bank may have investment discretion for an investment agency account, or it may provide investment advice for a fee with limited or no investment discretion. Investment agency accounts for which the bank has investment discretion or for which it provides investment advice for a fee are considered fiduciary accounts by the OCC and are subject to applicable sections of 12 CFR 9, Fiduciary Activities of National Banks.

In a discretionary investment agency account, the bank usually has sole authority to purchase and sell assets and execute transactions for the benefit of the principal, in addition to providing investment advice. The bank's investment authority is usually subject to investment policy guidelines established in the investment agency contract.

In some discretionary investment agency accounts, the bank is given limited investment authority. Major investment decisions, such as changing the account's investment strategy or asset allocation guidelines, might be subject to the principal's approval.

In nondiscretionary investment agency accounts, the bank may provide investment advisory services for a fee to the principal, but must obtain the principal's consent or approval prior to buying or selling assets. The bank may also be responsible for investment services such as executing investment transactions, disbursing funds, collecting income, and performing other custodial and safekeeping duties.

Mutual Fund Wrap Accounts

Many national banks offer separately managed accounts that invest in a select group of mutual funds instead of individual stocks and bonds. (See the next section for more information on mutual funds.) The client pays the bank a "wrap" fee based on the amount of invested assets in return for asset allocation modeling, mutual fund analysis and selection, and portfolio monitoring and reporting services. Wrap accounts have become quite popular over the past decade. The type offered by most national banks is a "packaged wrap program." Annual wrap fees, usually paid in arrears and billed quarterly, can range from 75 to 150 basis points. Wrap programs have minimum investment requirements starting at about $10,000.

In a typical "packaged" wrap account, the client or investment manager selects a model portfolio from 5 to ten alternatives. Computer modeling is generally used to design a series of model portfolios that theoretically offer the highest expected return for a given level of risk. The modeling program applies historical and expected future performance, historical risk, and the correlation coefficients of available asset classes to create different asset allocation mixes for different levels of risk. Asset allocation mixes are achieved through investment in selected mutual funds.

The client and the bank investment adviser establish the client's risk tolerance and specific investment objectives for the account. From this information, an appropriate portfolio is selected and the client's funds are invested in the mutual funds for each asset class. The bank selects the mutual funds for the wrap program and is usually responsible for re-balancing and reallocating the client's assets when warranted by changes in market conditions, return expectations, or the client's investment objectives and risk tolerance.

The SEC has adopted Rule 3a-4 under the Investment Company Act of 1940 (ICA) to provide a nonexclusive safe harbor from the definition of investment company for discretionary investment advisory programs, including wrap fee programs, that involve large numbers of clients. The rule provides that programs by which a large number of clients receive the same or similar advice will not be regulated under the ICA if they meet conditions designed to ensure that participating clients receive individualized treatment. In addition, programs that comply with the rule are not required to register the accounts that participate as publicly offered securities under the Securities Act of 1933.

Commingled or Pooled Investment Funds

A national bank may serve as the investment manager, or adviser, for various types of pooled investment funds. The most common are collective investment funds and open-end management investment companies (mutual funds). Other types of pooled investment funds include unit investment trusts, closed-end investment companies, and unregistered investment funds, such as private equity limited partnerships and hedge funds.

Collective Investment Funds (CIFs). CIFs are bank-administered trust funds designed to facilitate investment management by combining the assets of individual fiduciary accounts into a single investment fund with its own specific investment strategy. Although CIFs are similar to mutual funds, they have different tax, regulatory, and cost structures. CIFs remain a popular vehicle for investing the assets of smaller fiduciary accounts. See the *Comptroller's Handbook for Fiduciary Activities* for more information on CIFs.

Mutual Funds. Mutual fund is a term generally used to describe an open-end investment company that is registered with the Securities and Exchange Commission. This type of investment company pools money from its shareholders, invests in a portfolio of securities, and continuously offers to sell or redeem its shares to the public. The company's portfolio is managed by professional investment advisers to meet specific investment objectives. Many national banks and their affiliates provide investment management services for investment companies such as mutual funds. National banks also provide investment management services for clients who wish to invest in mutual funds and other types of investment companies.

The "Conflicts of Interest" booklet of the *Comptroller's Handbook* provides additional information relating to investing fiduciary portfolios in mutual funds and other types of investment companies.

Other Investment Services

Ancillary to its role as a fiduciary investment manager or adviser, a national bank may provide other types of fee-based investment services for its clients. For example, a bank might provide asset or business valuation, property management, and brokerage services for closely held businesses, real estate, and mineral interests. These activities are described in the *Comptroller's Handbook for Fiduciary Activities*.

Investment Clients

Personal Investors

National banks provide investment management services for persons through private trusts, investment agency accounts, tax-advantaged retirement accounts, and the various types of commingled funds. The characteristics of personal investors and the circumstances and opportunities that confront them are more diverse and complex than those of any other investor class. Each person's financial profile is unique, and many investors have a combination of taxable and nontaxable portfolios. Managers must also integrate estate planning into the investment program and often must work with other professionals to accomplish a client's goals.

Unlike institutional accounts, personal accounts are often managed on behalf of different generations, each with unique needs and objectives. Thus, asset

---

allocation strategies may need to address multiple objectives and multiple investment time horizons. Personal accounts often have unique assets: the family farm, stock in closely held companies, family residences, or mineral interests. In most cases, these types of assets have limited marketability, and clients may never want to sell them. They create additional risks and investment complications that the fiduciary portfolio manager must appropriately control and monitor.

Investment managers must understand how taxes can affect the overall asset allocation decision and portfolio construction process for personal accounts. Focusing on after-tax returns is a way to add value and gain competitive advantage. Incorporating a total portfolio approach, investment managers can use a host of strategies that are designed to enhance returns and to eliminate, reduce, or delay tax consequences. Financial derivatives are examples of investment tools that can be used to create customized tax strategies for clients.

A carefully planned investment policy for a personal account should incorporate the unique factors of that investor. Investment objectives should be clearly defined in terms of return requirements, risk tolerance, and constraints such as liquidity, time horizon, taxes, legal considerations, and other special circumstances. The investment policy should be embodied in an operational statement that specifies the actions that will achieve the investor's financial objectives

Institutional Investors

Institutional investors include company pension plans, investment companies, banks, insurance companies, business entities, governmental bodies, and endowments. They can be nonprofit or for-profit entities. Investment policy considerations can vary widely because of differing business, regulatory, and political environments.

Managing institutional portfolios is complex and challenging. Each portfolio requires a well-defined and appropriate investment policy. An investment manager's considerations are somewhat different when investing for an institution than when investing for a person. Among the factors that should be considered are the nature of the institution's fiduciary obligations to its employees and shareholders, its tax status, and other legal and regulatory requirements. The investment manager must understand these factors and incorporate them appropriately into the portfolio management process.

Retirement Plans

National banks manage investment portfolios established with tax-exempt funds contributed for retirement, savings, or welfare. A bank may serve as trustee or agent; in either role, the bank can be an investment manager or adviser. Retirement accounts include employee benefit plans and self-employed retirement trusts.

A corporate entity's defined benefit plan illustrates just how complicated managing a pension plan's portfolio can be. The objective of the pension plan combines the objectives of the plan sponsor, the pension plan itself, and plan beneficiaries. The plan's fiduciaries must develop a portfolio policy that reflects the plan's unique objectives, risk tolerance, constraints, and preferences. The most important objectives are to fund liabilities, avoid significant losses, and comply with applicable laws.

Investment Companies

National banks provide investment management services to public and private investment companies under a written contract. An investment company is an organization whose exclusive business is to own securities for investment purposes. It can be organized as a corporation, trust, partnership, association, joint-stock company, fund, or any other organized group of persons. An investment company raises money from investors who purchase ownership interests in the company. (These interests can be offered publicly or privately.) The company then invests the funds into a pool, or pools, of investment securities in accordance with established investment objectives.

Endowments and Other Nonprofit Organizations

Endowment funds are established to benefit a broad range of nonprofit institutions, including religious organizations, educational institutions, cultural entities, hospitals, private social organizations, trade associations, and corporate and private foundations. Endowment funds are long-term in nature, have a broad range of investment policy objectives, and are usually not taxable.

Developing an investment policy for an endowment fund requires a compromise between the sponsoring institution's demands for current income and the probabilities of achieving required rates of return on invested capital over time consistent with the fund's risk tolerance. An endowment's portfolio manager must assess a variety of risks and establish an appropriate investment policy.

Endowments that have adopted a total return approach to match their spending policies determine the required rate of return by summing the maximum spending rate and the expected inflation rate. This approach ensures the maintenance of the real value of the endowment if this total return objective is achieved over time.

Regulation and Supervision

The OCC requires national banks acting in a fiduciary capacity to invest fiduciary funds in a manner consistent with applicable law, as expressed in 12 CFR 9.11, Investment of Fiduciary Funds. Through its normal supervisory processes, the OCC assesses the risks created by fiduciary investment management services and ensures that national banks provide these services in a safe and sound manner and comply with applicable laws that fall under OCC jurisdiction.

Functionally Regulated Activities

The Gramm-Leach-Bliley Act of 1999 (GLBA) codified the concept of "functional regulation," recognizing the role of the Securities and Exchange Commission (SEC), the Commodities Futures Trading Commission, and state insurance commissioners as the primary regulators of securities, commodities, and insurance activities, respectively.

As the primary regulator of national banks, the OCC has the responsibility for evaluating the consolidated risk profile of a bank. This responsibility includes assessing the potential material risks posed by functionally regulated activities conducted by the bank or a functionally regulated entity (FRE), such as a subsidiary or affiliated SEC registered investment adviser (RIA). A key component of this assessment is evaluating a national bank's systems for monitoring and controlling risks posed by functionally regulated activities conducted in the bank or an FRE.

GLBA also modified the definition of "investment adviser" in the Investment Advisers Act of 1940 by narrowing the exemption from registration for national banks. Effective May 11, 2001, a national bank providing investment advice to a registered investment company must register with the SEC. The SEC is the functional regulator of an RIA.

A national bank can provide investment advisory services to registered investment companies through internal departments or divisions, a registered bank subsidiary, or a registered affiliated entity. If provided through an internal bank department or division, the bank may register itself or it may register the separately identifiable department or division (SIDD) responsible for providing investment advice to registered investment companies. If the activities are conducted in a SIDD, then the SEC regulates the activities subject to federal securities laws, and the OCC regulates the entity in relation to applicable banking law.

There are other ways that a national bank can provide investment management services that are functionally regulated by the SEC. For example, a national bank may employ an affiliated or unaffiliated RIA to provide investment management services for the bank's fiduciary accounts. If the RIA is a bank subsidiary, the subsidiary's activities can pose direct risks to the bank's earnings, capital, and reputation if not properly managed.

The OCC's primary supervisory focus with respect to a bank subsidiary or affiliated RIA is assessing the potential material risks that the adviser poses to the national bank and the effectiveness of the bank's oversight systems for monitoring and controlling those risks. The risk assessment will generally include a review of the following:

- The adviser's strategic plan and its impact on the bank;

- The significance of current and planned revenue from the adviser in relation to bank revenue;

- The amount of capital provided to and consumed by the adviser;

- The impact on the bank's liquidity from providing resources to the adviser either through direct funding or from reputation risk; and

- Systems for monitoring revenue sensitivity to changing market conditions at the adviser and bank levels.

The "General Procedures" section of this booklet beginning on page 77 contains supervisory guidance for assessing risk posed to a bank by a RIA. Additional guidance on functionally regulated activities can be found in the "Asset Management" booklet of the *Comptroller's Handbook*.

The OCC is the primary supervisor of a national bank's investment adviser activities that are not conducted by an RIA. National banks that manage or advise private trust accounts, collective investment funds, institutional accounts, personal investment portfolios, and other unregistered investment funds are not required to register as an investment adviser with the SEC. OCC examiners will assess the risks, risk management systems, and compliance with applicable law in national banks providing investment management services for these types of accounts.

Private Trusts

The investment authority, duties, and responsibilities of a national bank serving as a discretionary trustee for a private trust are derived from the governing trust document, applicable state trust statutes, federal law, trust common law, and judicial interpretations and decisions. A majority of states has adopted the prudent investor rule from the American Law Institute's 1992 *Restatement of the Law Third, Trusts*. This rule embraces the concepts of modern portfolio theory and risk management and applies them to trustees. An overview of trust investment law and the prudent investor rule is provided in appendix B of this booklet.

The OCC supervises a national bank's private trust investment activities through enforcement of 12 CFR 9, Fiduciary Activities of National Banks and safe and sound banking practices. Litigation involving trustees and beneficiaries of private trusts is administered through the appropriate state judicial system.

Employee Benefit Plans

Retirement accounts subject to the Employee Retirement Income and Security Act of 1974 (ERISA) must be managed to comply with the fiduciary investment standards established in the act, as well as the terms of the governing document. An overview of ERISA's fiduciary investment standards is provided in appendix C of this booklet. The OCC has an agreement with the U.S. Labor Department, the government agency responsible for administration and enforcement of ERISA, that establishes communication processes for referrals of potential violations of ERISA that are identified during OCC examinations.

Risks

Investment risk is commonly described by relating it to the uncertainty or the volatility of potential returns from a portfolio or investment over time. The source, probability, and impact of this uncertainty depend on the particular portfolio or investment. Sources of investment risk include financial exposure to changes in interest rates, equity and debt markets, inflation, foreign exchange rates, commodity prices, and other global economic and political conditions.

Investment risk is inherent in the individual portfolios and assets that a national bank fiduciary manages, or advises, for account principals and beneficiaries. These parties are the actual owners of the portfolios and the associated investment risk. A national bank's failure to manage its clients' investment risk in a prudent and loyal manner can increase a bank's level of transaction, compliance, reputation, and strategic risk and adversely impact earnings and capital.

Transaction Risk

Transaction risk is the current and prospective risk to earnings and capital arising from fraud, error, and the inability to deliver products or services, maintain a competitive position, and manage information. Transaction risk encompasses product development and delivery, transaction processing, systems development, computing systems, complexity of products and services, and the internal control environment. Transaction risk is also referred to as operating or operational risk. This risk arises every day as transactions are processed. It is a risk that transcends all divisions and products in a bank.

In managing investment portfolios, a bank must process a significant volume of transactions and must produce a great many reports. Both the transactions and reports are of many different types. For example, a bank may be required to:

- Execute and account for the purchase and sale of portfolio investments,
- Account for the receipt and distribution of investment income (dividends, interest, and capital gains distributions),
- Prepare investment valuations and performance measurement data,
- Pay expenses relating to investment property management,
- Execute contracts for clients and with third-party service providers,
- Prepare and distribute client portfolio reports, and
- Prepare and distribute management information reports.

Investment-related transactions are processed and reports are prepared for a wide range of investment products and services, as well as for clients with different characteristics, needs, and expectations. Portfolio investments may include all investable asset classes from domestic and foreign markets. Because of such investment variety and complexity, sophisticated and expensive information systems and product delivery channels are required, as well as strong internal controls that include contingency and disaster recovery plans.

Compliance Risk

Compliance risk is the current and prospective risk to earnings or capital arising from violations of or noncompliance with laws, rules, regulations, internal policies and procedures, or ethical standards. This risk exposes the institution to fines, civil money penalties, payment of damages or restitution, and the voiding of contracts. Compliance risk can lead to diminished reputation, reduced franchise value, limited business opportunities, reduced expansion potential, and an inability to enforce contracts.

A fiduciary portfolio manager must comply with the terms of the governing document (assuming such terms are legal) that establishes the fiduciary relationship, typically a trust or agency contract. A fiduciary portfolio manager must also comply with a multitude of federal, state, and local laws and regulations to which the bank and each individual client are subject. These include, but are not limited to, trust investment law, securities law, banking law, tax law, contract law, environmental law, consumer protection law, and criminal law. In addition, fiduciary portfolio managers must comply with applicable bank policies, procedures, and ethical guidelines.

The investment management compliance framework is complex and requires sound legal expertise, an ethical and highly trained staff, and an effective compliance program. The investment management business is exposed to the possibility of unauthorized conflicts of interest and self-dealing. A bank that does not comply with applicable law can suffer lawsuits, regulatory supervisory action, and severe damage to its reputation. The financial impact of litigation, regulatory action, and criminal activity is difficult to estimate, but it can be significant in relation to earnings and capital. In addition, such adverse situations may be highly publicized in the bank's market and damage a bank's reputation.

Strategic Risk

Strategic risk is the current and prospective impact on earnings or capital arising from adverse business decisions, improper implementation of decisions, or lack of responsiveness to industry changes. This risk is a function of the compatibility of an organization's strategic goals, the business strategies developed to achieve those goals, the resources deployed in support of these goals, and the quality of implementation. The organization's internal characteristics must be evaluated against the impact of economic, technological, competitive, regulatory, and other environmental changes.

The investment management business has become a primary source of profitability and shareholder value in many banks. The implementation of a successful investment management business requires a sound strategic planning process embraced by the board and senior management. It requires substantial provision of financial, human, and technological resources. Information systems, product development and distribution, and personnel expenditures must be appropriate for the diversity and complexity of an organization's operations. If they are not, the result may be poor earnings performance, wasted capital, and diminished shareholder value.

Reputation Risk

Reputation risk is the current and prospective impact on earnings and capital arising from negative public opinion. This affects the institution's ability to establish new relationships or services or to continue servicing existing relationships. This risk may expose the institution to litigation, financial loss, or a decline in its customer base. The assessment of reputation risk recognizes the potential impact of the public's opinion on a bank's franchise value. As the public's opinion of a bank deteriorates, the bank's ability to offer competitive products and services may be affected.

Success in providing investment management services depends on the quality of the bank's reputation with its current and prospective clients and the general marketplace. Investors are more demanding in terms of expected investment performance, product selection, information reporting, service, and the use of advanced technology. Clients are also concerned with their own reputation and expect bank fiduciary investment mangers to act loyally and prudently in protecting it through proper management of their assets.

A bank's reputation in the marketplace depends on its ability to effectively manage transaction, compliance, and strategic risks, as well as the financial risks within each individual portfolio. Litigation, regulatory action, criminal activity, inadequate products and services, below average investment performance, poor service quality, and weak strategic initiatives and planning can lead to a diminished reputation and, consequently, to an inability to compete and be successful.

Risk Management Processes

Effective risk management requires an understanding of the specific needs and risk tolerance of clients and the bank, as well as the types and characteristics of portfolios and assets managed or advised by the bank. Risk management processes must be developed and implemented that effectively assess, control, and monitor the risks affecting each of these entities. The client's needs, objectives, and risk tolerance can differ from those of the bank, and the bank's processes should recognize and appropriately address these differences. Risk managers must be cognizant of and sensitive to these potential conflicts when implementing risk strategies and internal controls.

This section describes how national banks should manage the risks associated with providing investment management services. Specific processes for managing investment risk of individual portfolios are addressed in appendix A, "Portfolio Management Processes." Additionally, the *Comptroller's Handbook for Fiduciary Activities* provides risk management processes applicable to individual investments held in fiduciary portfolios.

An effective risk management system is characterized by active board and senior management risk supervision and sound processes for risk assessment, control and monitoring.

Risk Supervision

A bank's board of directors and senior management must fully support and oversee the risk management process for investment management services, including risk management processes related to functionally regulated activities. The following are the key responsibilities of a board and senior management relating to investment management services:

- ***Establish strategic direction, risk tolerance standards, and an ethical culture consistent with the bank's strategic goals and objectives.***

The board of directors and senior management should establish a supervisory environment that communicates their commitment to risk management and a sound internal control system. They must give investment management strategic direction by approving strategic and financial operating plans. Senior business line managers use the strategic plan as guidance for developing long-term and short-term financial plans, policies, internal controls, staffing levels, and information systems. Management's philosophy and operating style should be effectively communicated and understood by all employees.

The board of directors, senior management, and business line managers should establish a risk management culture that is consistent with the company's risk tolerance and promotes an ethical environment. The goal is to create a cultural environment dedicated to effective risk management and fulfilling fiduciary responsibilities to clients.

The investment management organization should have a code of ethics and established standards of conduct for its employees' internal and external activities, including personal trading rules. The standards should be clearly communicated to all employees. Compliance with the standards should be monitored and enforced.

- ***Establish an appropriate organizational structure with clear delineation of authority, responsibility, and accountability through all levels of the organization.***

An investment management group under the direction of a chief investment officer (CIO) typically supervises fiduciary investment organizations in larger national banks. In some banks, the responsibility may lie with a formalized

---

committee, such as an investment policy committee of which the CIO is a member. The investment management group may consist of representatives from the bank's various fiduciary divisions, elements of senior management, and representatives from the bank's risk management group (if the group exists). Portfolio managers, research analysts, traders, operational units, and information technology units generally report to the CIO. Each of these bodies may have its own internal operating structures and processes.

The investment management group may supervise all fiduciary investment activities. The group may be required to approve policies, procedures, and investment strategies that will be implemented by line managers and other personnel. It may establish subgroups, or committees, charged with specific areas of responsibility. For example, there may be committees that establish equity and fixed income strategies, manage trading activities, or manage asset allocation modeling programs.

- **Develop and implement a comprehensive and effective risk management system.**

There is no standard way to organize a risk management system. The formality and structure of a risk management system should be consistent with a bank's structure and diversity of operations. Each institution should tailor its risk management program to its own needs and circumstances.

In large banks, the investment management operation may have a separate risk management function as part of the bank's corporate-wide risk management organization. The corporate risk management organization may be structured to include senior managers, line managers, and personnel from compliance, audit, legal, operations, human resources, information systems, and product development divisions.

To enhance risk management capabilities, the process should have common processes and risk-related terminology. Using the same terminology facilitates communication across functions, divisions, departments, and business units, as well as up or down the management hierarchy.

- **Monitor the implementation of investment management risk strategies and the adequacy and effectiveness of risk management processes.**

The board of directors, its designated committees, and senior management must effectively oversee and monitor the financial performance of the

---

investment management organization and the effectiveness of risk management processes. Well-designed monitoring processes will enable the board and senior management to effectively evaluate the investment management organization's performance in achieving its strategic objectives and financial operating goals. Although risk management, audit, and compliance groups may provide testing and monitoring support, the responsibility and liability for deficient risk monitoring rests with the board and senior management.

Risk Assessment

As previously discussed in the "Risks" section, investment risk comes from many sources. Effective risk management requires that investment risk specific to a particular portfolio and the risks a bank assumes when managing investment portfolios be identified and understood. Risk assessment processes help determine what the risks are, how they should be measured, and what controls and monitoring systems are needed.

Persons assigned the responsibility of managing risk must identify the types of risk and estimate the levels of risk created by investment management services. Business line, portfolio, and other risk managers must understand the characteristics and expectations of the bank's different types of clients and portfolios and identify the applicable risks. Managers can then estimate the level of risk to the client and the bank.

Internal and external risk assessment should be comprehensive and continual. In order to facilitate the identification and understanding of relevant risks, the bank should clarify what type of risk measurement and reporting processes it expects from portfolio managers, third-party service providers, and investment counter parties.

Risks vary over time because of changes in clients' characteristics and needs, portfolio composition, capital markets and economies, political environments, and bank strategies. Therefore, some risk assessments should be ongoing or open-ended, others should take place regularly, and some should take place when significant changes occur.

Economic Research and Capital Market Analysis

The investment organization should have access to timely and competent economic analyses and forecasts for the capital markets in which its clients will be investing. Larger banks may have economic and securities research units that continually monitor global economics and capital markets. Smaller investment organizations with fewer internal resources may acquire this expertise from third-party service providers, including other national banks.

Whatever the source, these functions provide necessary forecasts of capital market expectations, currency relationships, interest rate movements, commodity prices, and expected returns of asset classes and individual investment instruments. These forecasts and recommendations help the organization establish appropriate investment policies and strategies, select appropriate investments, and manage risk effectively.

Pre-acceptance Account Reviews

The initial assessment of investment management risk and reward is fundamental to sound portfolio management. The process of reviewing a client's characteristics and investment portfolio prior to acceptance of a fiduciary investment management mandate must be thorough and complete in all respects. The approval authority must ensure that the types of clients and investment portfolios accepted are consistent with the bank's risk strategies and are authorized by policy. Risk managers must ensure that the bank has the requisite resources and expertise (or can obtain the expertise at reasonable cost) to appropriately manage the portfolio.

Investment Performance Measurement and Analysis

The application of performance measurement processes depends on the type of account, the bank's fiduciary responsibilities, and the needs of the client. Performance measurement systems calculate the return on a portfolio and various portfolio segments over a specified time. Because of rapid advances in information technology, the methods of calculating, analyzing, estimating, and reporting investment performance are increasingly sophisticated and reliable.

The investment management industry is standardizing the presentation of investment performance and moving to disclose information fully in a fair, consistent, and understandable manner. A benefit of using a standardized method of calculating and reporting investment returns is that senior management can better monitor and evaluate each portfolio manager's performance. Standardized performance measures also enable portfolio managers to better compare their investment performance with that of external managers that use similar investment styles. Finally, standardized measurement and reporting enhances a client's ability to understand investment results and make comparisons between service providers.

The Association for Investment Management and Research (AIMR) promotes fair representation and full disclosure of investment performance for its members and the industry in general. AIMR has developed comprehensive performance presentation standards for its members that have become widely accepted and used by the industry. The standards, which include acceptable methods of calculating and reporting investment performance, provide an industry yardstick for evaluating fairness and accuracy in investment performance presentation. While the OCC does not officially endorse these standards or require national banks to adopt them, the OCC considers them to be good guides for national banks that are constructing investment performance measurement and reporting systems.

Some examples of questions that a performance measurement system should be able to answer are:

- What is the portfolio's total return and risk over a specified period, and did it meet or exceed the portfolio's needs and objectives?

- How does the return break down into capital gains, dividends, interest, currency fluctuations, etc?

- To what extent does asset allocation, market timing, currency selection, industry sector, or individual asset selections explain performance?

- How does the portfolio's risk-adjusted returns compare with those of its benchmark?

- How does a portfolio manager's investment performance compare with that of a competing universe of managers?

- Is there evidence of exceptional expertise in a particular market or investment style?

- Have risk diversification objectives been achieved?

Whether a bank needs a performance measurement system that answers each of these questions depends on its size, complexity, and regulatory environment. A bank has the flexibility to establish a performance measurement system that is appropriate for its particular needs and financial resources.

To measure investment performance, a firm periodically values a portfolio and calculates its rate of return over a specific time frame. Because performance measurement is based on transactional data, it is important that the data be accurate, reliable, and consistent. A huge amount of valuation and transaction information is synthesized into a few performance return measures. If performance measurements and risk assessments are to be useful, portfolios must be valued frequently and accurately.

A portfolio's performance can be attributed to many decisions, including the choice of instruments, markets, currencies, individual securities, and portfolio managers. Given this complexity, a detailed and frequent analysis of performance is prudent. Persons responsible for managing investment risk should periodically assess the performance of each account and portfolio manager. Evaluations of the portfolio manager should analyze the investment risks taken and should conclude whether he or she has managed these risks appropriately and professionally.

The investment management industry standard for calculating investment return is a **time-weighted, total return** measure. Time-weighted returns minimize the impact of external cash flows (over which the portfolio manager has little or no control) on the rate of return. For time periods longer than one year, the return is calculated as an annual return, or a compounded average annual return. Portfolio rates of return can be computed daily, monthly, quarterly, and annually and then compared with a portfolio's goals and objectives, which may include designated benchmarks.

A **benchmark** is the standard of comparison for investment performance analysis. It is a passive representation of the portfolio's investment strategy against which actual performance can be measured. The benchmark may be a passive market index, such as the S&P 500, a mean return of a universe of actively managed funds, or a customized portfolio of securities that closely resembles a portfolio manager's style or a client's normal portfolio strategy.

Benchmarks are discussed more fully in appendix A, "Portfolio Management Processes."

Investment risk and return measures should be analyzed to gain a true measure of relative portfolio performance. There are many risk measures used by portfolio managers and analysts. Some of the more common are standard deviation of returns, modified duration, beta, tracking error, value-at-risk, and down-side risk measures such as relative semi-variance. Portfolio risk managers must understand the strengths and weaknesses of any measure used and verify that the measures accurately capture the risk being assessed.

Risk-adjusted returns are used to measure the relative performance of investment portfolios and their managers. Risk-adjusted returns can also highlight investment performance that a portfolio manager achieves by incurring misunderstood, mispriced, unintended, or undisclosed risks. Risk-adjusted return measures also permit a more meaningful comparison of a portfolio manager's performance with that of an appropriate benchmark or a required rate of return.

Examples of risk-adjusted return measures are the Sharpe Ratio, the Treynor Measure, the Jensen Alpha, the Information Ratio, and the Sortino Ratio. It is important that the risk-adjusted return measure used captures the appropriate performance information and relevant risks. With any risk-based return statistic, the portfolio manager must understand how it is calculated, what risk is captured, the time periods involved, and how the statistic is to be used.

Many investment management firms complete periodic **performance attribution analyses** on their portfolios. Risk managers evaluate the investment decisions that cause performance to deviate from established benchmarks. A performance attribution analysis facilitates two kinds of analysis by enabling managers to identify the separate components of return from active management and to measure the risks associated with accessing these return streams.

A **return attribution analysis** looks at the performance of a portfolio to determine whether the key determinant of return is, for example, asset allocation, sector selection, or security selection. **A risk attribution analysis** looks at the sources of risk and the volatility of returns in the portfolio to determine how and to what degree these risks affect portfolio performance. Risk managers also use risk attribution analyses to monitor whether a portfolio manager is adhering to a stated investment strategy or style and to measure aggregate risk factors from multiple portfolios. Portfolio managers can use risk attribution analysis to make sure they are not taking more of a given risk than their limits allow and to ensure that risks are appropriately diversified.

Stress testing can be performed to ascertain how the risk profile of portfolios and individual assets will behave under various conditions. Risk managers can test the likely impact of various market conditions or other circumstances on the value of an instrument, portfolio, or strategy. These circumstances include changes in risk factors, correlations, or other key assumptions and unusual events such as large market moves. Stress tests are useful when portfolios have instruments whose returns are not normally distributed — that is, are nonsymmetrical. Such instruments include options, structured notes with embedded options, range notes, and other derivative instruments. If a portfolio's returns are approximately linear, stress testing may not be necessary.

Stress tests are performed using scenario, historical, simulation or random sampling (Monte Carlo analysis) formats. Relevant stress tests include how risk and return change when different assumptions or modeling techniques are used. Emphasis should be placed on stress testing significant risks. Stress tests can consider all types of leverage and related cash flows, including loans, options, structured notes, futures, and forwards. Managers can test both the impacts of large market moves and combinations of small market moves to identify those that are likely to affect the portfolio. Events that would breach such investment policy guidelines as risk tolerance limits, asset allocation ranges, or investment instrument restrictions should be monitored and addressed.

If an organization uses stress testing, the process should be consistent and well defined. If appropriate, tests should be performed at least quarterly and whenever material events occur at the aggregate fund and individual portfolio level, incorporating asset/liability issues as relevant. Material events include significant changes in the market, a significant shift in a portfolio's strategy or composition, and a change in managers. Stress test results should be periodically back-tested to see whether the process would have accurately forecasted past performance, especially previous market shocks.

Back-testing is a practice of applying historical data to an investment valuation, simulation, or forecasting model. When back-testing a model, a bank uses the model's historical accuracy as an indication of its forecasting accuracy. A model's historical performance can be compared with its expected performance; an instrument's performance can be compared with the predictions for it; and an investment strategy's performance can be compared with the forecasts of a simulation. Back-testing can assess expected risk, return, and correlations. It can also help verify the robustness of an estimate.

Assessing model risk is an important element of managing portfolios. Investment organizations use many different models for valuing, forecasting, and analyzing markets, portfolios, and individual securities. Examples of models used for individual securities are dividend discount, multi-factor, duration, and option valuation models. A model is only as good as the quality of its data and the expertise of its users. Risk managers should continually assess and validate models used in the investment management process. Refer to OCC Bulletin 2000-16, "Risk Modeling," for guidance on validating computer-based financial models. The guidance outlines sound model validation principles and processes.

Risk assessment is a difficult, but necessary, endeavor in the investment management business. The investment management organization should regularly assess its risk management strategies for portfolios to ensure that it is achieving the best results possible for its clients. Portfolio risk managers have many tools to choose from, each of which has its strengths and weaknesses. Some are extremely quantitative and difficult to use; others are too theoretical and don't reflect real-world behavior and performance. Managers must decide which tools are most relevant and useful for the organization.

Risk Controls

Risk controls are policies, procedures, processes, and systems established to control risk. Such controls are essential to the investment management organization. They help maintain risk at levels consistent with the organization's risk tolerance. They ensure that strategies are appropriate for each client's circumstances. The bank should have a comprehensive program of controls for managing client portfolios and the risks affecting the investment management organization.

Risk control is especially important with regard to fiduciary responsibility and liability. For purposes of this booklet, risk controls are structured under the headings of policies, procedural control processes, personnel, information technology and reporting systems, and product development and distribution. Although this section may not address every area in the investment management organization requiring controls, it outlines the general controls such organizations require.

Policies

The investment management organization should have approved written policies and documentation standards that support its risk management objectives and strategies. Appendix D of this booklet describes the policy standards required by 12 CFR 9.6. In addition, 12 CFR 12.7 requires a national bank to adopt policies and procedures for securities trading activities. Appendix G of this booklet also provides a list of items to consider when developing an investment management policy.

Written policies should express the investment philosophy and risk tolerance of the investment management organization and provide comprehensive standards, risk limits, operating procedures, and control processes. Detailed policy guidelines and operating procedures for the varying investment divisions or groups within the overall organization should be established and followed. Business managers and other risk management support groups should monitor and enforce policy compliance.

Policies should be specific to the types of client portfolios and asset classes managed by the bank. They should be consistently applied through all levels of the organization. Definitions should be written and accompanied by relevant examples. Written definitions are beneficial and reduce the likelihood of incomplete communication, ambiguities, and misinterpretations. Common terms that could require definition include risk, hedging, speculation, derivative, complex, leverage, benchmark, average maturity, government security, and high quality. Descriptors such as material, relevant, and significant should also be defined.

Policies should apply to both internal and external portfolio managers and should be applied consistently across similar asset classes and strategies. All employees affected by the policies and procedures should receive copies of them and should confirm in writing that they have read and understood them. Employees should receive copies of policy updates or changes promptly, and an appropriate re-confirmation program should be established. Policies should include specific provisions for notifying senior management immediately of any loss or change in key personnel.

Management should establish a formal process to review and amend the policy if appropriate. The review process should be outlined in the policy and address events such as changes in business strategies, products, services, systems and risk tolerance. Policy should be reviewed at least annually and more frequently if appropriate. The board or its designated committee should review and approve the policy annually.

Procedural Control Processes

Account review procedures. Before accepting a fiduciary investment relationship, the bank must review the prospective account to ensure that the bank has the expertise and systems to properly manage the account and achieve the client's needs and objectives. The bank should establish a due diligence process for reviewing a prospective client's portfolio. The due diligence review should consider applicable risk management issues and ensure compliance with appropriate policies and procedures. The process should be fully documented to prevent inadequate or inconsistent reviews and poor decisions.

There should be a formal, documented process for accepting fiduciary investment management accounts, whether as trustee or agent, after completing the due diligence review. A fiduciary investment committee, or trust committee, typically administers the account acceptance process.

Following an account's acceptance, the portfolio's assets should be formally reviewed and an appropriate investment policy should be established for the account. Each account should be reviewed regularly, at which time its performance and investment policy should be evaluated. Refer to appendix D for specific information on the requirements established for fiduciary account reviews by 12 CFR 9.6. Procedures should be in place to ensure compliance with this section of the regulation.

Fiduciary authority and responsibility. All managers should be subject to consistent investment management agreements, objectives, and guidelines. Account documents should clearly specify the bank's fiduciary obligations and articulate the nature and limits of each party's status as agent or principal. Policies and procedures should specify in writing the capacity of committees or individuals authorized to sign agreements on behalf of the bank with clients and other third parties.

The possibility of lawsuits claiming that a party did not adequately perform its fiduciary responsibilities should motivate banks to articulate and document fiduciary assignments as well as to monitor compliance carefully. Each time a client's investment guidelines or directives are changed, or a new portfolio manager is assigned, the portfolio should be reviewed to determine if the bank's fiduciary responsibilities should be re-defined and re-documented.

Internal risk limits. The organization should establish limits on relevant risks for investment instruments, individual portfolios, and the aggregate portfolio. Often, risk limits are expressed in notional terms. Other limits are expressed through measures of risk such as duration, tracking error, or value-at-risk. Examples of items that can be limited include credit and market risk exposures, tracking error relative to a benchmark, duration risk relative to a benchmark, industry concentration, or the percentage of a portfolio that is illiquid or dependent upon theoretical models. Risk limits should be meaningful in the current portfolio and market environment, and should not be constructed solely from historical data and experience. Risk limits, of course, may reduce expected returns. Portfolio managers should understand this risk/return tradeoff.

Separation of duties and functions. There should be independent oversight of all major investment activities and reasonable separation of operational duties and functions. Organizational and functional charts that address the responsibilities of business lines and support groups should be compared to determine whether there are conflicts of interest, inadequate checks and balances, unassigned responsibilities, or unofficial authority. Function charts should specify who is authorized to do what and who is not. An organizational chart should specify the reporting lines for risk management, compliance, and internal audit groups. It should also identify other checks and balances that are important controls.

Portfolio and asset valuation. Procedures should be established for valuing portfolios and individual assets. These tasks can be performed internally as long as there are appropriate checks and balances and independent verification. Valuation may be delegated to an external portfolio manager, custodian, or pricing service after appropriate procedures, quality controls, and checks and balances are established. Valuation should comply with any statutory or regulatory valuation standards established for a particular type of client or asset.

The methods of valuation and the frequency of valuations depend on the investment instrument. Valuation should be documented, understood, compliant with written policies and operating procedures, and used consistently within the organization. The bank must ensure that the valuation processes of sub-advisers, custodians, and other subcontractors are compatible with those of the bank and that they meet applicable fiduciary standards.

Readily priced instruments such as publicly traded securities, exchange-listed derivatives, and many over-the-counter securities and derivatives can be priced daily. These instruments are often tracked and priced by exchanges, data vendors, brokers, and dealers. Market prices can be obtained electronically or in hard copy. Portfolio positions can be valued, or marked to market, on the basis of such quotes.

Less-readily priced instruments such as complex CMOs, exotic derivatives, many private placement notes, and other custom instruments should be priced as often as possible, preferably weekly. Often, the values of less-readily priced instruments provided by dealers, custodians, and third-party pricing services are based on theoretical models. Banks should make the model and pricing mechanism for these instruments explicit and available so their accuracy can be independently verified.

Some investments such as real estate, closely held businesses, and unregistered investment funds are not readily priced. It may be difficult to obtain frequent and reliable valuations on such assets. Methods of valuing these investments include appraisals, theoretical financial models, committee estimates, and single-dealer quotes. Valuation methods should be explicit, and their accuracy should be independently verifiable. Valuations should be performed as frequently as feasible and whenever a material event occurs. "Material" should be clearly defined and the primary valuation factors for these assets should be determined. Any change in the primary valuation factors or any material event should trigger a valuation update.

Risk managers should document the accuracy and reliability of all valuation processes and data sources and ensure that valuations are completed as required by internal policies and procedures, third-party contracts, and regulatory reporting standards. For all investment types, risk managers should determine whether the pricing source could be motivated to inflate or deflate valuations.

The ultimate authority on valuation for each instrument type should be determined and named in writing. Exceptions to any valuation procedures should be identified and reported under established policies. Senior management approval should be required for any valuation process that relies on the portfolio manager who controls the asset.

Differences in valuations between a bank's records and valuation sources should be reconciled under established procedures at least monthly, or more frequently if differences are material. If consistent valuation procedures are applied, most price differences can usually be explained by error, bid/offer spread adjustments, timing differences, or valuation overrides.

Overrides are adjustments made by a manager to valuations provided by independent parties under established valuation procedures. Typically, managers override independent valuations during periods of market dislocation when they believe those valuations are incorrect. Although their beliefs at times may be well founded, all overrides should be reported and investigated if the differences in valuation are material.

Procedures should be established that set forth the circumstances in which valuations can be overridden, who should be notified of each override, and who should approve each override. These procedures should be communicated to all relevant parties. In addition, management should continually track and review the number and magnitude of overrides to confirm that all material adjustments have been investigated and that practices are consistent with the override policy.

Personnel

Successful implementation of business strategies and risk management requires a knowledgeable and responsible management group and well-trained and capable professionals in the front office, middle office, and back office. To effectively manage personnel, the investment organization must address staffing needs, compensation programs, third-party investment delegation practices, and broker selection criteria.

Staffing. Attracting talented people to a firm and systematically developing, motivating, and retaining them is a challenge and should be a fundamental management strategy. Management development and succession plans are essential because of the keen competition for successful portfolio managers

---

and business executives. Offering employees rewarding careers that provide challenging opportunities, fair and consistent performance evaluations, competitive compensation packages, and management development and training programs is essential. Appropriate investment management training should be provided to all personnel employed by the investment management organization.

Compensation. Banks that wish to remain competitive in investment management must be prepared to pay their managers well. Banks may tie part of an individual's compensation to individual effort and achievement, but may also link compensation to other factors such as performance comparisons with another unit in the bank or external peer groups. An individual's compensation may also be linked to the success of the entire investment management organization.

Risk managers should determine whether the bank's and each portfolio manager's compensation is structured in accordance with the client's needs. For example, the compensation structure should encourage the manager to follow the portfolio's investment strategy. If properly structured, performance-based compensation can be an effective way of focusing a portfolio manager's attention on meeting or exceeding a portfolio's investment objective. How and when such fees are calculated should be controlled and monitored to ensure that appropriate fiduciary investment standards are preserved.

Performance-based compensation may be charged provided that such arrangements are:

- Constructed in accordance with applicable law;
- Addressed in the governing document or contract (specifically the basis of calculation and circumstances under which the fees will or will not be payable); and
- Disclosed in a written statement to each principal or beneficiary whose interest will bear the fee.

Appropriate legal counsel should be sought for all such arrangements.

Third-party investment managers and advisers. If authorized by applicable law, fiduciary portfolio managers may decide that delegating investment authority is prudent. The investment organization should have formal

---

procedures for selecting and monitoring third-party investment managers and advisers. Refer to appendix B, "Trust Investment Law," for a comprehensive discussion of fiduciary delegation issues and standards. Appendix F, "Guidelines for Selecting Investment Managers and Advisers," provides guidance on selection criteria.

Broker selection. Fiduciary investment managers are usually responsible for selecting brokers to execute securities transactions for clients. Performance is measured after transaction costs, and a fiduciary is required to seek "best execution" for client transactions. "Best execution" refers to executing client securities transactions so that the client's total cost, or proceeds, in each transaction is the most favorable under the particular circumstances at that time.

The bank should have policies and procedures to assess, select, and monitor brokers that will execute investment security trades. The board of directors, or its authorized entity, should review and approve brokerage placement policies, procedures, and management's list of authorized securities brokers. A fiduciary investment management organization must institute and follow a thoroughly documented process for pursuing best execution for its clients.

Obtaining the lowest commission should not, by itself, determine which broker is chosen to execute a transaction. The quality of execution is an important determinant when selecting brokers. Managers should consider the following when selecting brokers to execute securities transactions:

- Execution capability,
- Commission rates and other compensation,
- Financial responsibility,
- Responsiveness to the investment manager, and
- Value of services provided, including research.

Managers should consider the ability of the broker to fulfill commitments by assessing the broker's capital, liquidity, operating performance, and general reputation in the industry. The organization should obtain and review any available information about the broker from other broker customers, regulators, and self-governing organizations of the securities industry such as the National Association of Securities Dealers.

In larger banks, the performance of brokers is often tracked and rated using a formalized point scoring system. While such practice is not required and not

As of May 17, 2012, this guidance applies to federal savings associations in addition to national banks.*

feasible in many smaller institutions, a bank must document each broker's performance and demonstrate that the bank's selection process is prudent and effective. The authorizing body should review the list of approved brokers periodically and should update it at least annually. Periodic reviews by auditors and compliance personnel are appropriate and validate the integrity of the selection and monitoring process.

Refer to the "Conflicts of Interests" booklet of the *Comptroller's Handbook* and the *Comptroller's Handbook for Fiduciary Activities* for information relating to brokerage soft dollar arrangements and risk management processes for securities trading activities.

Information Technology and Reporting Systems

Data and information systems. An effective risk management system requires a large variety and volume of relevant data. Data must have high integrity and be integrated with respect to historical returns, current positions, and the analytics being undertaken. Many large banks manage globally diversified portfolios that require multi-currency accounting and reporting systems. The systems must keep track of each day's transactions and provide a valuation of each account based on current market prices around the world, computed in one base currency, or reference currency. The base currency is the currency in which the client chooses to have the portfolio valued. Every item, including stocks, bonds, and cash, must be included in the accounting and reporting system.

Division managers, portfolio managers, and client service officers should use a management information system that generates portfolio information reports either in hard copy or on-line. Most computer-based portfolio management systems allow the user to perform asset allocation modeling, investment simulation, compliance monitoring, re-balancing, trading interface, benchmarking, client statement preparation and presentation, real-time valuation, and investment risk analysis.

Internal reporting and exception tracking. If a bank is to manage all risks effectively, reporting must be adequate. Reports should accurately and comprehensively cover all assets and accounts under management. The bank must communicate portfolio investment information and presentation material to appropriate staff members. Examples of information that should be considered for dissemination are:

- Portfolio valuation and investment performance reports,
- Approved security investment lists,
- Asset allocation modeling portfolios and criteria,
- Investment policy exception reports,
- Equity and fixed income statistics and commentary,
- Economic and capital markets statistics and commentary, and
- Marketing presentation materials.

The development of a portfolio valuation and performance measurement system requires sophisticated computer software capable of processing a mass of data and summarizing it in a few performance figures. The diversity of instruments, quotation and trading techniques, and information sources renders the analysis susceptible to errors. However, a responsible investment organization must be able to master the process. Numerous companies have developed ready-made performance software that can be linked to an organization's accounting system.

Effective risk control requires an early warning system for problems and violations. Management should specify what positions, risks, and other information should be reported, how often, and to whom. It is crucial to rely on established reports and procedures, rather than culture or individuals, to sound the alarm. Processes should establish which violations of risk policies, guidelines, or limits require exception reports, who is responsible for monitoring and reporting exceptions, and to whom they must be reported.

Portfolio managers should be required to periodically verify that investment performance reports are accurate and that investment policy compliance statements are updated whenever a material change occurs. This process should be accompanied by random or other internal reviews of investment activity and portfolio holdings to verify compliance with investment policy.

Exception policies should also include what corrective actions should be taken and by what date, who will monitor the corrective actions, and who is authorized to make exceptions to the exception policy. A typical escalation procedure requires progressively more senior staff to be notified of unresolved exceptions or exceptions that are increasing.

Independent personnel should oversee the exception reporting and follow-up process. If that is not possible or practicable, adequate checks and balances should be established. Management must ensure that all personnel are subject to consistent requirements on performance reporting, exception reporting, and escalation procedure requirements.

Client reporting. Investors also want improved risk and performance reporting. Most investment management organizations do an adequate job of reporting performance relative to benchmarks, but can improve their reporting of how the firm manages risks, what its tracking error to benchmark is, and how risk is measured and monitored. The institutional market has seen a sharp increase in requests to provide detailed risk management reporting with periodic performance reporting. The investment management group should issue client performance reports that are consistent with industry standards and that meet client demands. It is also important that the reported benchmark is appropriate for the account and understood by the client.

Contingency and disaster recovery plans. Contingency and disaster recovery plans are crucial. Financial interruptions such as market trading halts and failures of systems, communications, and power have proven the need for effective contingency and disaster recovery plans. Contingency plans should address all essential functions and operations and should be coordinated with the bank's overall contingency planning process.

Contingency and disaster recovery plans are also necessary for third-party fiduciary service providers, custodians, and other subcontractors. Each business unit and service provider should conduct trial runs to test the adequacy of its plans as well as the adequacy of the plans of those on whom they rely, whether these plans are to be implemented by trained internal staff or a specialty firm.

A disaster plan should include access to duplicate records of investment inventory, legal title to positions, master counterparty agreements, authorities, and scheduled cash inflows and payments. It should prepare the organization to resume operations off-site in a reasonable time if the primary location shuts down. The plan should ensure access to contingency financing in a liquidity crisis.

Product Development, Assessment, Marketing, and Distribution

Broadening the product line to generate growth is a common strategy in the investment management business, and multi-product firms are growing in number and significance. Because investment performance of asset classes tends to run in cycles, a broad product line can insulate a firm against temporary problems in one or more areas. But merely offering a broad array of products does not guarantee success, especially in the institutional market. Firms should offer only as many products as they can efficiently provide without diluting their standard of performance; each product must achieve competitive performance and profitability goals.

To compete and grow, many banks must offer and deliver investment products and services globally. Providing global investment services creates many challenges for product development and distribution, but also creates opportunity to generate new revenues by offering broader investment options, geographical reach, and specialized expertise. Offering global investment services is expensive and requires openness to change and new ways of thinking. Banks that wish to operate global investment businesses must ensure that they have the appropriate management expertise, client demand, financial resources, and information systems to succeed.

Normally, no new instrument, asset class, product, or service should be introduced without adequate due diligence. Products and services created through joint ventures and other types of affiliations with third parties should follow this rule. The review process should set forth the risk and return dimensions on which the new business or product will be evaluated and should require the manager to submit all relevant information. Approving authorities should consider such characteristics as managerial skill and whether the new business or product will require changes in valuation methods, back-office/settlement facilities, counterparties, oversight, methods of executing trades, authorities/resolutions, and reporting capabilities.

Many banks have formed new-product committees. This type of forum can provide an important risk control mechanism by including representatives from the business line, operations, legal, compliance, tax, and risk management divisions. New-product committees can ensure that risks associated with new products are appropriately identified and effectively controlled to ensure a smooth product rollout.

A growing number of firms, rather than adding to their own product offerings, form strategic alliances and sub-advisory relationships (third-party investment delegation) to fill gaps in their product line. This is an appropriate strategy for firms that, although lacking efficient product development and distribution processes, maintain strong relationships with clients. A firm must select reputable, high-quality partners with the resources and commitment to deliver. All parties in an alliance should agree explicitly about what the product's characteristics should be, how much it should cost, and what reports will be required.

Risk Monitoring

Risk monitoring processes are established to evaluate the performance of the bank's risk strategies and control processes in achieving the bank's and its clients' financial goals and objectives. Risk monitoring should be a coordinated effort of the entire risk management organization.

Risk managers should perform frequent, independent reviews of compliance with risk policies, procedures, control systems, and portfolio management practices. Noncompliance with established policies and procedures should be addressed through corrective action plans that are fully documented and communicated to affected parties. Managers should ensure continuing compliance with their clients' investment policy guidelines, governing documents, and other applicable law.

In monitoring risk, the bank should independently verify compliance with risk policies and other requirements at least annually for both aggregate risk and the risk in individual portfolios. Such compliance should also be independently verified whenever a material change or exception occurs. Portfolio managers can be required to notify risk managers of any material change and affirm in writing at least annually that they are in compliance with these requirements and other investment guidelines. This can be part of the 12 CFR 9.6 annual account review process.

Compliance monitoring of individual portfolio guidelines should be an ongoing and possibly daily task. The frequency depends on the nature of the guidelines, the complexity of accounts, and the diversity of operations. Portfolio management software that is now available and widely used automates such compliance controls and monitoring.

Risk managers should review periodic performance attribution analyses of risk and return to verify that portfolio activity is consistent with the stated investment strategy and to monitor for style drift. Style drift refers to the tendency of an investment manager offering a specific investment style to change that style over time. Marked deviation from the performance of other managers using similar styles or strategies should be identified, evaluated, and reported to risk managers, if appropriate. Risk managers should also review account investment policy to ensure that it remains consistent with the client's goals and objectives, which may change over time.

Risk managers should review methods of valuation, performance measurement systems, and modeling programs and related systems. A risk management or audit group can perform this review. Reviews should follow established procedures and be documented to reflect their scope and completion. These reviews should be specific to investment instruments, asset classes, and individual portfolio manager styles. Some considerations are:

- Appropriateness,
- Comparability with others,
- Quality of data and assumptions,
- Thoroughness of independent verifications,
- Valuation calculations and methods, and
- Quality and usefulness of output and related reporting.

Risk Management Function

A risk management function can help business line managers monitor and assess risks. Its primary objective should be to identify and help control business risks that exceed tolerances established in strategic plans, policies, and operational control procedures. An effective risk management function identifies deficiencies in risk controls and monitoring and makes recommendations to improve policies, procedures, controls, risk-taking strategies, products and services, risk assessment tools, and training programs. Refer to the "Asset Management" booklet of the Comptroller's Handbook for additional information on risk management functions.

Control Self-assessments

Control self-assessments are internal processes in which business units assume the primary responsibility for broadly identifying key business and operational risks and evaluating and establishing appropriate control systems. The reviews evaluate risk and monitor adherence to policies, operating procedures, and other control processes. Self-assessments help managers improve their ability to manage risk by strengthening their understanding of risks that directly affect their areas of responsibility.

Compliance Program

The investment management organization should have a compliance program to monitor compliance with law, internal policies, and risk limits, internal controls systems, and client documents. For large and broadly diversified organizations, a formal compliance program is encouraged. For smaller, less complex organizations, less formalized programs may be appropriate. The program's formality should be determined by an assessment of risk and organizational resources.

The compliance program should:

- Have the strong support of the board and senior management.
- Be administered by a designated compliance officer.
- Establish procedures for periodic compliance testing and validation.
- Make business line management responsible and accountable for compliance and the compliance program's effectiveness.
- Establish effective and timely communication systems for reporting and following up on compliance activity and deficiencies.

Audit Program

An audit function is essential to effective risk management and internal control monitoring. Investment management services should be included in the coverage of the company's audit program, if it is a significant activity. Results of investment management audit activity should be effectively communicated to the appropriate managers. Deficiencies in internal controls and risk management processes should be addressed through written corrective action plans and effectively monitored for adequate follow-up and resolution.

Examination Procedures

The following expanded procedures provide detailed guidance on how to examine investment management services provided by a large bank. The procedures are consistent with and supplement the minimum core assessment standards in the "Large Bank Supervision" booklet of the *Comptroller's Handbook*. The procedures can be used, as needed, in community banks to supplement the core assessment and examination procedures in the "Community Bank Fiduciary Activities Supervision" booklet of the *Comptroller's Handbook*.

The expanded procedures include sections for assessing the types and level of risk posed to a bank by functionally regulated activities conducted by the bank or by an RIA, as may be the case. Beginning on page 77 you will find a separate set of expanded procedures for conducting a risk assessment of a bank's RIA subsidiary or an RIA directly owned by the bank's holding company that provides investment advisory services to the bank.

The use of expanded procedures should be coordinated with the asset management examiner responsible for planning and coordinating all asset management supervisory activities for the bank being examined. The examiner's assessment of risk, the supervisory strategy's objectives, and any examination scope memorandum should determine which of this booklet's procedures should be performed to meet examination objectives. Seldom will every objective/step of this booklet's procedures be required.

General Procedures — Bank Activities

Objective: Develop a preliminary assessment of the quantity of risk and the quality of risk management relating to investment management services. The assessment should address the types and level of risk from functionally regulated activities conducted by the bank or an RIA subsidiary or affiliate. It should be used to establish the scope of examination activities for investment management services, including the examination of individual asset classes managed in fiduciary investment portfolios, if appropriate.

1. Determine the types and characteristics of investment management products, services, and distribution channels by obtaining and reviewing the following, if applicable:

    ❑ OCC information databases.

    ❑ Previous reports of examination, analyses, related board and management responses, and work papers.

    ❑ The asset management profile.

    ❑ OCC correspondence files.

    ❑ Call reports.

    ❑ Supervisory reports issued by other functional regulators.

    ❑ Bank risk monitoring reports from the board, committees, business lines, functionally regulated entities, risk management groups, compliance, legal, and audit functions.

2. Discuss the following with the organization's key risk managers:

    •   Significant investment management risk issues and management strategies;
    •   Significant changes in strategies, products, services, and distribution channels, including functionally regulated activities conducted by the bank or its subsidiaries;

- Significant changes in organization, policies, controls, and information systems; and
- External factors that are affecting investment management services.

3.   Develop a preliminary risk assessment and discuss it with the asset management and bank examiners-in-charge (EIC) for perspective and strategy coordination. Consider the following:

- Previous examination conclusions and recommendations;
- Internal risk and control assessments;
- Strategic and business plans;
- New products, services, and distribution channels; and
- Changes in organization, policies, procedures, controls, and information systems.

If the bank provides investment management services through an entity for which the OCC is not the primary functional regulator, discuss the supervisory approach that should be taken with the asset management EIC and bank EIC before establishing the examination strategy for investment management services. For further guidance on functional supervision, refer to the "Bank Supervision Process" and "Asset Management" booklets of the *Comptroller's Handbook* and OCC Memorandum 2000-19, dated August 8, 2000.

Objective: Establish the examination objectives, scope, and work plans to be completed during the supervisory cycle.

1.   Based on the preliminary risk assessment, and in consultation with the bank and asset management EICs, as well as other appropriate regulatory agencies, establish the objectives, scope, and specific work plans for the examination of investment management services during the supervisory cycle. Prepare and submit a final planning memorandum for approval by the bank EIC that includes the following information:

- A preliminary business and risk assessment profile of investment management services. Refer to the "Asset Management" booklet for guidance.

- Examination activity objectives for the supervisory cycle including a description of the products and services to be reviewed.

- The types of examination activities (on-site and quarterly monitoring), examination schedules, and projected workdays for the examination.

- The scope of examination procedures to be completed during each activity, including risk-oriented sampling guidelines. The memorandum should address how much testing or direct verification may be necessary. The scope of examination activity and selected procedures should be consistent with the risk assessment and focus on the bank's higher-risk portfolio management activities. Examples of higher-risk accounts include those holding the following types of investments:

  - Proprietary investment products;
  - Alternative investments such as private equity funds, hedge funds, and structured investment products;
  - Closely held businesses and real estate; and
  - Large asset concentrations, including own bank stock.

- The necessary examiner resources to complete the activities.

- The types of communication planned, such as meetings and final written products.

2. Complete the following procedures after receiving the EIC's approval of the planning memorandum (these procedures should be performed in close consultation with and with authorization from the asset management EIC):

- Select the asset management examination staff and make assignments consistent with the objectives, scope, and time frames of the planned examination activities;

- Discuss the examination plan with appropriate bank personnel and make suitable arrangements for on-site accommodations and additional information requests; and

---

- Contact each member of the examination team and provide necessary details concerning examination schedules and his or her individual assignment responsibilities.

Note: If necessary, refer to the "Examination Planning and Control," "Large Bank Supervision," and "Asset Management" booklets of the *Comptroller's Handbook* for additional information on planning these and other related examination activities.

Quantity of Risk — Bank Activities

Transaction Risk

Conclusion: **The quantity of transaction risk from investment management services is (low, moderate, high).**

Objective: To determine the quantity of transaction risk from the bank's delivery and administration of investment management services.

1. Obtain and analyze management information reports relating to transaction processing and reporting within the investment management organization. Consider the following structural factors:

   - The volume, type, and complexity of transactions, products, and services offered through the bank;
   - The condition, security, capacity, and recoverability of systems;
   - The complexity and volume of conversions, integrations, and system changes;
   - The development of new markets, products, services, technology, and delivery systems to maintain competitive position and gain strategic advantage; and
   - The volume and severity of operational, administrative, and accounting control exceptions and losses from fraud and operating errors.

2. Analyze and discuss with management how the following factors affect the quantity of transaction risk related to investment management services:

   - The impact of strategy, including marketing plans and the development of new markets, products, services, technology, and delivery systems;
   - The impact of acquisition and divestiture strategies; and
   - The maintenance of an appropriate balance between technology innovation and secure operations.

3. Analyze and discuss with management how the following factors affect the quantity of transaction risk related to investment management services:

    - The impact of external factors including economic, industry, competitive, and market conditions; legislative and regulatory changes; and technological advancement;
    - The impact of infrastructure threats on the bank's ability to deliver timely support and service; and
    - The ability of service providers to provide and maintain service level performance that meets the requirements of the bank.

4. Obtain the results of the bank information systems examination relating to investment management services. Analyze and discuss the conclusions and recommendations with the assigned examiner(s).

5. Obtain the results of the fiduciary operations and internal control examinations, if applicable. Analyze and discuss the findings and recommendations relating to investment management services with the assigned examiner(s).

6. If applicable, obtain and analyze the results of the supervisory review of the bank's RIA activities. Consolidate the review's transaction risk assessment into the overall assessment of the bank's transaction risk from investment management services.

7. Reach a conclusion on the quantity of transaction risk from investment management services based on the findings of these and other applicable asset management examination activities.

Compliance Risk

Conclusion: The quantity of compliance risk from investment management services is (low, moderate, high).

Objective: To determine the quantity of compliance risk from the bank's delivery and administration of investment management services.

1. Select an appropriate sample of accounts for which the bank acts as a discretionary portfolio manager or provides investment advice for a fee. Accounts should be selected on a basis consistent with the examination's planning memorandum. Refer to the "Sampling Methodologies" booklet of the *Comptroller's Handbook* for additional guidance on appropriate sampling techniques.

2. Review each selected account for compliance with relevant investment management criteria established in:

    *   The governing instrument or contract;
    *   Federal, state, and local law and regulation;
    *   The account's investment policy statement, if available;
    *   Internal policies, procedures, and control processes; and
    *   Contracts with third-party service providers.

3. Obtain and analyze the types and level of policy exceptions, internal control deficiencies, and law violations that have been identified and reported internally. Review information from the following sources:

    *   ❑ Board and committee minutes and reports.
    *   ❑ Risk management division reports.
    *   ❑ Compliance reports.
    *   ❑ Control self-assessment reports.
    *   ❑ Internal and external audit reports.
    *   ❑ Regulatory reports.
    *   ❑ Other OCC examination programs.

4. Obtain and analyze the types and volume of litigation and consumer complaints related to investment management services.

---

5. Discuss significant litigation and complaints with management and determine the risk to capital and the appropriateness of corrective action and follow-up processes. If necessary, refer to the "Litigation and Other Legal Matters" booklet of the *Comptroller's Handbook* for additional procedures.

6. If applicable, obtain and analyze the results of the supervisory review of the bank's RIA activities. Consolidate the review's compliance risk assessment into the overall assessment of the bank's compliance risk from investment management services.

7. Reach a conclusion on the quantity of compliance risk from investment management services based on the findings of these and other asset management examination activities. Consider the following factors:

    • The nature and extent of business activities, including new products and services;

    • The volume and significance of noncompliance and nonconformance with policies and procedures, laws, regulations, prescribed practices, and ethical standards; and

    • The amount and significance of litigation and customer complaints.

Strategic Risk

Conclusion: Aggregate strategic risk from investment management services is (low, moderate, high).

Objective: To identify and estimate strategic risk inherent in the bank's delivery and administration of investment management services.

1.   Obtain and analyze the bank's strategic plan for investment management services by considering the following strategic factors:

- The magnitude of change in established corporate mission, goals, culture, values, or risk tolerance;
- The financial objectives as they relate to the short- and long-term goals of the bank;
- The market situation, including product, customer demographics, and geographic position;
- Diversification by product, geography, and customer demographics;
- Past performance in offering new products and services;
- Risk of implementing innovative or unproven products, services, or technologies;
- Merger and acquisition plans and opportunities;
- Potential or planned entrance into new businesses, product lines, or delivery channels; and
- The implementation of new systems.

2.   Discuss with management and reach conclusions about the impact of external factors on strategic risk. Consider the following:

- Economic, industry, and market conditions;
- Legislative and regulatory change;
- Technological advances; and
- Competition.

3.   Obtain and analyze conclusions from the investment management services' "Quality of Risk Management" examination procedures. Incorporate those conclusions into the evaluation of strategic risk from investment management services. Consider the following factors:

- The expertise of senior management and the effectiveness of the board of directors;
- The priority and compatibility of personnel, technology, and capital resources allocation with strategic initiatives;
- Past performance in offering new products or services and evaluating potential and consummated acquisitions;
- Performance in implementing new technology or systems;
- The effectiveness of management's methods of communicating, implementing, and modifying strategic plans, and consistency with stated risk tolerance;
- The adequacy and independence of controls to monitor business decisions;
- The responsiveness to identified deficiencies in internal controls; and
- The quality, integrity, timeliness, and relevance of reports to the board of directors necessary to oversee strategic decisions.

4. If applicable, obtain and analyze the results of the supervisory review of the bank's RIA activities. Consolidate the review's strategic risk assessment into the overall assessment of the bank's strategic risk from investment management services.

5. Reach a conclusion on aggregate strategic risk from investment management services.

Reputation Risk

Conclusion: Aggregate reputation risk from investment management services is (low, moderate, high).

Objective: To identify and estimate reputation risk from the bank's delivery and administration of investment management services.

1. Discuss with management the impact of the strategic factors listed below on reputation risk from investment management services:

    - The volume and types of assets and number of accounts under management or administration;
    - Merger and acquisition plans and opportunities; and
    - Potential or planned entrance into new businesses, product lines, or technologies (including new delivery channels), particularly those that may test legal boundaries.

2. Discuss with management the impact of the external factors listed below on reputation risk from investment management services:

    - The market's or public's perception of the corporate mission, culture, and risk tolerance of the bank;
    - The market's or public's perception of the bank's financial stability;
    - The market's or public's perception of the quality of products and services offered by the bank; and
    - The impact of economic, industry, and market conditions; legislative and regulatory change; technological advances; and competition.

3. Obtain and analyze conclusions from the investment management services "Quality of Risk Management" examination procedures. Incorporate those conclusions into the evaluation of reputation risk from investment management services. Consider the following factors:

    - Past performance in offering new products or services and in conducting due diligence prior to startup;
    - Past performance in developing or implementing new technologies and systems;

- The nature and amount of litigation and customer complaints;
- The expertise of senior management and the effectiveness of the board of directors in maintaining an ethical, self-policing culture;
- Management's willingness and ability to adjust strategies based on regulatory changes, market disruptions, market or public perception, and legal losses;
- The quality and integrity of management information systems and the development of expanded or newly integrated systems;
- The adequacy and independence of controls used to monitor business decisions;
- The responsiveness to deficiencies in internal control;
- The ability to minimize exposure from litigation and customer complaints;
- The ability to communicate effectively with the market, public, and media;
- Policies, practices, and systems protecting information customers might consider private or confidential from deliberate or accidental disclosure; and
- Management's responsiveness to internal, external, and regulatory review findings.

4. If applicable, obtain and analyze the results of the supervisory review of the bank's RIA activities. Consolidate the review's reputation risk assessment into the overall assessment of the bank's reputation risk from investment management services.

5. Reach a conclusion on aggregate reputation risk from investment management services.

Quality of Risk Management — Bank Activities

Conclusion: The quality of risk management for investment management services is (strong, satisfactory, weak).

Policies

Conclusion: The board has adopted (strong, satisfactory, weak) investment management policies.

The following are the core assessment standards applicable to risk management policies that should be considered when completing these examination procedures:

- The consistency of policies with the bank's overall strategic direction and with policies in the rest of the organization.
- The structure of the bank's operations and whether responsibility and accountability are assigned at every level.
- The reasonableness of definitions that determine policy exceptions and guidelines for approving policy exceptions.
- The periodic review and approval of policies by the board or an appropriate committee.
- The appropriateness of established risk limits or positions and whether periodic revaluation is required.
- The structure of the compliance operation and whether responsibility and accountability are assigned at every level.

Objective: To determine the adequacy and effectiveness of policies for investment management services.

1. Identify and obtain policies for investment management services, including those related to information systems and functionally regulated entities, and, if applicable, distribute the policies to examiners responsible for examining the business lines in investment management services, including separate investment classes.

2. Review policy documents and determine whether they

- Are formally approved by the board, or a designated committee(s);

- Address applicable law including 12 CFR 9.5 and 12.7;

- Outline investment management goals and objectives, investment philosophy, fiduciary responsibilities, ethical culture, risk tolerance standards, and risk management framework;

- Address all significant products and services including

  - The types and size of acceptable accounts;
  - A list and description of investment products and styles;
  - Compensation schedules;
  - Descriptions of marketing and distribution channels; and
  - How new products and services are developed and approved.

- Address the organizational structure and supervisory framework by establishing

  - Organizational and functional charts;
  - Defined lines of authority and responsibility;
  - Delegation authority and approval processes;
  - Processes to select, employ, and evaluate legal counsel;
  - Standards for dealings with affiliated organizations; and
  - Personnel practices.

- Establish comprehensive portfolio management processes that include appropriate guidelines for

  - Reviewing and accepting accounts and performing periodic portfolio reviews;
  - Economic and capital market analyses and reporting;
  - The development and implementation of portfolio investment policy programs;
  - Securities trading and broker placement; and
  - Selecting and monitoring third-party service providers.

- Address information systems and technology applications, such as

  - Accounting and other transaction record keeping systems;

- Management information system requirements;
- Portfolio management software that provides appropriate valuation, performance analysis, simulation, and trading interface applications and abilities;
- Securities trading systems; and
- Systems security and disaster contingency plans. Consider the following OCC documents:

  - ❑ OCC Bulletin 97-23, "FFIEC Interagency Statement on Corporate Business Resumption and Contingency Planning";

  - ❑ OCC Bulletin 98-3, "Technology Risk Management";

  - ❑ OCC Bulletin 98-38, "Technology Risk Management: PC Banking";

  - ❑ OCC Bulletin 99-9, "Infrastructure Threats from Cyber-Terrorists";

  - ❑ OCC Bulletin, 2000-22, "Standards for Safeguarding Customer Information";

  - ❑ OCC Banking Circular Banking 226, "End-User Computing"; and

  - ❑ OCC Banking Circular 229, "Information Security."

- Establish appropriate information reporting and risk monitoring processes that include

  - Internal investment performance and risk management reporting standards;
  - Policy exception tracking and reporting processes;
  - Client reporting guidelines;
  - Control self-assessment processes;
  - Portfolio stress-testing, back-testing, and model validation processes;
  - Customer complaint resolution procedures; and
  - Performance reviews of third-party service providers including securities brokers.

- Establish a compliance program by including

  - A description of the program's purpose, responsibility, and accountability;
  - Operating and testing procedures;
  - Reporting and follow-up requirements and processes; and
  - Educational material and resource references.

- Include appropriate guidelines for

  - Communicating policies and subsequent policy changes;
  - Monitoring policy compliance and reporting exceptions; and
  - Policy review and approval by the board, or its designated committee, at least annually.

3. Evaluate the policy review process and determine whether changes in risk tolerance, strategic direction, products and services, or the external environment are adequately and effectively reviewed.

4. Through discussion with management and other examiners, identify parts of the policy requiring development or revision. Consider the following:

   - Recently developed and distributed products and services;
   - Discontinued products, services, organizational structures, and information systems; and
   - Recent updates or revisions to existing policies and procedures.

5. Draw a conclusion on the adequacy and effectiveness of policies for investment management services.

Processes

Conclusion: Management has adopted (strong, satisfactory, weak) processes for investment management services.

The following are the core assessment standards applicable to risk management processes that should be considered when completing these examination procedures:

- The adequacy of processes that communicate policies and expectations to appropriate personnel.
- The production of timely, accurate, complete, and relevant management information.
- The adequacy of processes and systems to approve, monitor, and report on compliance with policy.
- The appropriateness of the approval process for policy exceptions.
- The adequacy of internal control including segregation of duties, dual control, authority commensurate with duties, etc.
- Management's responsiveness to regulatory, industry, and technology changes.
- The incorporation of project management into daily operations (e.g., systems development, capacity planning, change control, due diligence, and outsourcing).
- The adequacy of processes defining the systems architecture for transaction processing and for delivering products and services.
- The effectiveness of processes developed to ensure the integrity and security of systems and the independence of operating staff.
- The adequacy of system documentation.
- The adequacy of processes to ensure the reliability and retention of information (e.g., data creation, processing, storage, and delivery).
- The quality of physical and logical security to protect the confidentiality of customer and corporate information.
- The capabilities of the front and back office systems to support current and projected operations.
- The adequacy of corporate contingency plans and business resumption plans for relevant data centers, file servers, PCs, networks, service providers and business units.
- The adequacy of contracts and management's ability to monitor relationships with third-party service providers.
- The development of information technology solutions that meet the needs of end users.
- The capacity to deliver timely services and to respond rapidly to normal service interruptions or to attacks and intrusions from external sources.

- Whether risk measurement systems are appropriate to the nature and complexity of activities, and how these systems are incorporated into the decision-making process.
- The adequacy of processes assimilating legislative and regulatory changes into all aspects of the company.
- The commitment to allocate appropriate resources to training and compliance.
- The extent to which violations or noncompliance are identified internally and corrected.
- The adequacy of integrating compliance considerations into all phases of corporate planning, including the development of new products and services.

Objective: To determine the adequacy and effectiveness of supervision by the board, senior management, and business line management.

1. Determine how investment management services are organized and whether clear lines of authority, responsibility, and accountability are established through all levels of the organization. Obtain and evaluate the following:

   - Bank bylaws and resolutions.
   - Strategic plan and business strategies, including those related to functionally regulated entities.
   - Board and management committees, charters, minutes, and reports.
   - Management structures, authorities, and responsibilities.
   - Other organizational structures.

2. If the board has delegated investment management supervision to one or more committees, review each committee's composition, charter, meeting frequency, attendance, information reports, and board reporting processes for consistency with board guidance and regulatory requirements.

3 Evaluate the bank's strategic planning process for investment management services. Consider the following:

   - Does the process require the formulation and adoption of a long-term strategic plan supported by short-term business plans?

- Are planning processes for investment management services part of the bank's overall strategic and financial planning processes?

- Does the process require periodic assessment, updating, and re-affirmations by the board and management of investment management services strategic plans?

- Does the process consider all significant elements of risk that affect investment management services, such as internal risk tolerance standards, the corporate ethical culture, available financial resources, management expertise, technology capabilities, operating systems, competition, economic and market conditions, and legal and regulatory issues?

- Does the planning process for investment management services evaluate and determine the amount of capital necessary to support the business?

- Does the process include an effective means of communicating strategies, financial performance goals, and risk tolerance standards?

4. Evaluate how management implements the strategic plan and monitors and reports performance to the board, or its designated committee. Consider the following:

- Are policies and procedures consistent with the strategic plan?

- Are the development, implementation, and monitoring of short-term business plans consistent with board-established planning processes?

- Are management processes adequate and effective?

- Does management submit periodic reports to the board, or its designated committee, that provide accurate, reliable, understandable, and relevant information about the following:

  - Success in meeting strategic goals and objectives;
  - Quantity and direction of investment management services risks;
  - Adequacy of risk management systems;

- Financial performance analyses, including the adequacy of capital allocated to the business lines; and
- Summaries of changes to risk and business strategies, corrective actions, and proposed recommendations to address excessive risk levels or remedy control weaknesses.

5.   Reach a conclusion on the quality of board and management supervision of investment management services, including functionally regulated entities and forward the results to the appropriate asset management examiners.

Objective: To determine the adequacy and effectiveness of processes used to review and accept fiduciary investment portfolio accounts.

1.   Evaluate the due diligence process for reviewing potential fiduciary investment management accounts or portfolios. Determine whether the process considers the following:

- Terms of the governing instrument;
- Types of assets currently in the portfolio;
- Types of assets to be purchased and managed for the portfolio;
- Environmental due diligence reviews;
- Input from portfolio managers, risk managers, and legal consultants;
- Ability to appropriately manage the portfolio.

2.   Evaluate the processes for accepting or rejecting a potential account or portfolio, including the requirements of 12 CFR 9.6(a) for pre-acceptance reviews, by determining whether

- Time frames and approval mechanisms established for each step of the process are appropriate and followed;
- All appropriate information from the account due diligence review is made available for consideration;
- The process is formalized and adequately documented; and
- The process complies with internal policies and procedures.

Objective: To determine the adequacy and effectiveness of processes used to develop and approve client investment policy programs.

1.   Evaluate the initial post-acceptance review process required by 12 CFR 9.6(b). Determine whether the process includes

- A review of the governing instrument and a determination of its purpose, intent, investment guidelines, and powers;

- An evaluation of the characteristics and needs of account principals and beneficiaries;

- An evaluation of the portfolio's current assets for appropriateness and ability to manage;

- A review of prior portfolio management and performance; and

- A determination of compliance with internal policies and procedures.

2. Evaluate the process for determining and documenting the portfolio's investment objectives. Does the process

   - Articulate the account's risk tolerance?
   - Clearly establish investment goals and return requirements?
   - Adequately detail the account's status with regard to applicable law, liquidity, time horizons, taxes, and any other pertinent circumstances of its principals and beneficiaries?

3. Determine whether the process for establishing and documenting a portfolio's investment policy is adequate and effective by considering whether:

   - A written investment policy statement is required and appropriately agreed to by all parties involved.

   - The process includes, if appropriate, the following information:

     - Account purpose and background;
     - Investment objectives and constraints;
     - Investment policy guidelines, including asset allocation;
     - Investment class guidelines and performance benchmarks;
     - Guidelines for selecting investment managers and advisers;
     - Control and monitoring processes; and
     - Timing and content of client reports.

4. Evaluate processes for developing and implementing asset allocation modeling programs and selecting asset allocation guidelines for portfolios. Consider the following:

    •   The types and responsibilities of committees or groups established to manage the asset allocation modeling process;

    •   Whether processes and programs for developing and applying asset allocation portfolio models include

        –   Asset class and sector definitions and selection criteria,
        –   Asset class and sector construction,
        –   Investment instrument/category selection criteria and placement,
        –   Asset class/sector weighting criteria, and
        –   Risk measurement tools and their application;

    •   The types of research, analysis, and support for risk, return, and other assumptions and inputs used in the process;

    •   The types and adequacy of support for any statistical measures used in the process; and

    •   The methods used to adjust asset allocation models when economic conditions and client characteristics change.

5. Evaluate the processes used to select, construct, and apply performance benchmarks. The evaluation should consider

    •   The types and characteristics of benchmarks used;

    •   The methods used to select and construct benchmarks;

    •   Whether selected benchmarks have portfolio objectives and risk tolerance standards similar to those established for account investment policies; and

    •   Portfolio manager understanding of benchmarks and their appropriate use.

Objective: To determine the adequacy and effectiveness of processes used to implement an account's investment policy.

1.   If the bank delegates investment management authority, review the processes used to select and monitor third-party investment managers or advisors. Reach a conclusion about the adequacy and effectiveness of the processes by considering the following:

- Due diligence processes for selecting a third-party investment manager or adviser. Is there a thorough evaluation of all available information about the company? Consider the following:

    - Organizational and financial background.
    - Investment methodology and performance.
    - Risk management processes.
    - Management background.
    - Compensation policies.
    - Reporting capabilities.

- Third-party monitoring processes. Determine whether monitoring is routine and whether, when appropriate, the persons who monitor:

    - Review information reports provided by the company;
    - Review portfolios regularly to ensure adherence to established investment policy guidelines;
    - Analyze the company's financial condition at least annually and more frequently when increased risk is present;
    - Evaluate the cost of the relationship;
    - Review independent audits reports of the company; and
    - Perform on-site quality assurance reviews and test the company's risk management controls.

2.   Evaluate the processes by which individual investments for the portfolio are selected and acquired. The evaluation should consider

- Processes used to research, value, and estimate rates of return and correlations for potential investments;

- Processes used to value portfolio assets and account for portfolio transactions;
- Portfolio trading systems and controls including brokerage placement processes that assess, control, and monitor a broker's

  - Capability and performance in executing and settling trades,
  - Service value based on execution, pricing, and commission rates,
  - Financial ability, reputation, and commitment,
  - Quality of consulting and research services, and
  - Desire to cooperate in resolving differences.

- Processes used to review custodian appraisal and transaction reports.

3. Evaluate the processes used to re-balance portfolios, if applicable. Determine whether the process is

   - Formalized, continuous, and appropriately controlled, and
   - Consistent with bank policy, portfolio investment policy, and other procedural guidelines.

4. Analyze processes used to assess portfolio investment performance and reach conclusions on the quality of the following:

   - Account review processes. Determine whether processes are adequate and effective by considering their

     - Frequency,
     - Content,
     - Documentation standards, and
     - Compliance with bank policy and the annual review required by 12 CFR 9.6(c).

   - Reviews that ensure that portfolios adhere to the portfolio objectives and guidelines established in the investment policy. Does the process include adequate interim reviews that determine whether portfolios adhere to asset allocation and sector guidelines and how well portfolios perform relative to established benchmarks?

   - The types and application of investment return measurement tools.

- The types and application of investment risk measurement tools.

- The types of information obtained from clients and the types and frequency of communication with clients.

5. Evaluate the adequacy and effectiveness of risk reporting and exception tracking processes. Does the division maintain comprehensive management reports relating to investment performance, risk levels, and policy exception identification and follow-up? Examples of appropriate information include

    - Total return over relevant time periods;
    - Total return breakdown and attribution;
    - Achievement of portfolio objectives and performance comparisons with benchmarks;
    - Risk-adjusted return comparisons over relevant time periods;
    - Exceptions to investment policy guidelines and the status of follow-up; and
    - Exceptions to internal policies and procedures and the status of follow-up.

Objective: To determine the adequacy and effectiveness of internal control processes within the various units comprising the investment management services organization.

1. As appropriate and approved by the bank EIC and internal control examiner, select and complete appropriate internal control examination procedures from the "Large Bank Supervision" and "Internal Control" booklets of the *Comptroller's Handbook*.

2. After completing the examination procedures selected above and reviewing the internal control findings of other related fiduciary examination programs, draw conclusions on internal control for investment management services using the following format:

	Strong	Satisfactory	Weak
Control Environment	☐	☐	☐
Risk Assessment	☐	☐	☐
Control Activities	☐	☐	☐

Accounting, Information, and Communication	☐	☐	☐
Self-assessment and Monitoring	☐	☐	☐

The overall system of internal control for investment management services is

Strong	**Satisfactory**	**Weak**
☐	☐	☐

3.   Submit the final assessment of internal control to the examiner responsible for evaluating internal control for asset management activities.

Objective: Determine the adequacy and effectiveness of processes used to develop and approve new products, services, or lines of business.

1.   Evaluate how management plans for and develops new products and services. Consider the following:

- Types of market research conducted, such as product feasibility studies;
- Cost, pricing, and profitability analyses;
- Risk assessment processes;
- Legal counsel and review;
- Role of risk management and audit functions;
- Information systems and technology impact; and
- Human resource requirements.

2.   Evaluate the product approval process by selecting a sample of products or services developed and rolled out since the last examination of this area:

- Is the approval authority clearly established and adhered to?
- Were bank policies and procedures adequately followed?
- Does the process require adequate documentation of the factors considered and support for the final decision?

Personnel

Conclusion: The bank has (strong, satisfactory, weak) personnel for investment management services.

The following are the core assessment standards applicable to personnel that should be considered when completing these procedures:

- The depth of technical and managerial expertise.
- The appropriateness of performance management and compensation programs.
- The appropriateness of management's response to identified deficiencies in policies, processes, personnel, and control systems.
- The level of turnover of critical staff.
- The adequacy of training.
- The ability of managers to implement new products, services, and systems in response to changing business, economic, or competitive conditions.
- The understanding of and adherence to the strategic direction and risk tolerance as defined by senior management and the board.

Objective: To determine the adequacy of investment management services management and supporting personnel.

1. Review the experience, education, and other training of managers and key supporting personnel. The review should include portfolio managers, research analysts, traders, business line managers, and other personnel who manage risk. Determine whether personnel are

   - Adequate to the risks presented by the bank's investment management services. Consider the following:

     - Types and complexity of discretionary portfolios;
     - Types and complexity of investments managed;
     - Compatibility with investment management services and corporate strategic initiatives; and
     - Types and complexity of information processing and reporting systems.

- Knowledgeable about investment management policies, strategic plans, and risk tolerance standards.

- Aware of the bank's code of ethics, if applicable, and whether they demonstrate a strong commitment to high ethical standards.

2. Review recent staffing analyses prepared for applicable investment management services business lines and evaluate the adequacy of staffing levels by considering

- Current strategic initiatives and financial goals;
- Current business volume, complexity, and risk profile; and
- The impact of company-initiated cost-cutting programs, if applicable.

3. Compare job descriptions of managers and key supporting personnel with their experience, education, and other training (considering responsibilities they have that are not in their job descriptions). Determine whether personnel

- Are qualified and adequately trained for positions and responsibilities.

- Do not perform tasks outside their job descriptions that lower their overall performance or increase the bank's risks.

Objective: To determine the adequacy and effectiveness of the bank's personnel policies, practices, and programs.

1. Determine whether lines of authority and individual duties and responsibilities are clearly defined and communicated.

2. Evaluate the bank's investment management recruitment and employee retention program by reviewing the following:

- Recent success in hiring and retaining high-quality personnel;
- Level and trends of staff turnover, particularly in key positions; and
- The quality and reasonableness of management succession plans.

3. Analyze the investment management compensation and performance evaluation program by determining whether:

    • The compensation and performance evaluation program is appropriate for the types of products and services offered.

    • The program is formalized and periodically reviewed by the board and senior management.

    • The program is consistent with the bank's risk tolerance and ethical standards.

    • Responsibilities and accountability standards are clearly established for the performance evaluation program.

    • The program is applied consistently and is functioning as intended.

    • The program rewards behavior and performance that is consistent with the bank's ethical culture, risk tolerance standards, and strategic initiatives.

    • The program gives the board an adequate mechanism with which to evaluate management performance.

4. Review the investment management training program by considering the following:

    • The types and frequency of training and whether the program is adequate and effective;

    • How much of the investment management services budget is allocated to training and whether the financial resources applied are adequate; and

    • Whether employee training needs and accomplishments are a component of the performance evaluation program.

Objective: To determine the adequacy and effectiveness of third-party service provider selection and monitoring processes.

1. Review policies and procedures for the selection and monitoring of third-party service providers, including functionally regulated subsidiaries and affiliates. Discuss the process with management and document significant weaknesses in risk management. Consider the following in reaching conclusions:

    - The quality of the due diligence review process;
    - The contract negotiation and approval process;
    - Risk assessment processes;
    - Risk management and audit division participation;
    - Vendor monitoring processes, such as the assignment of responsibility, the frequency of reviews, and the quality of information reports reviewed; and
    - Vendor problem resolution process.

    Refer to OCC Advisory Letter 2000-9, "Third-Party Risk," for a discussion of appropriate risk management processes for third-party vendors.

Control Systems

Conclusion: The bank has (strong, satisfactory, weak) control systems for investment management services.

The following are the core assessment standards applicable to risk management control systems that should be considered when completing these examination procedures:

- The timeliness, accuracy, completeness, and relevance of management information systems, reports, monitoring, and control functions.
- The scope, frequency, effectiveness, and independence of the risk review, quality assurance, and internal/external audit functions.
- The effectiveness of exception monitoring systems that identify, measure, and track incremental risk exposure by how much (in frequency and amount) the exceptions deviate from policy and established limits, and corrective actions.
- The independent testing of processes to ensure ongoing reliability and integrity (e.g., Internet penetration testing).
- The adequacy of systems to monitor capacity and performance.
- The adequacy of controls over new product and systems development.

- The independent use and validation of measurement tools.

Objective: To determine the adequacy and effectiveness of investment management control and monitoring systems.

1.   Determine and evaluate the types of control and monitoring systems used by the board and management. Consider the following:

   - Board and senior management risk monitoring processes;
   - Risk management groups;
   - Committee structures and responsibilities;
   - Management information systems;
   - Quantitative risk measurement systems;
   - Compliance programs;
   - Control self-assessment processes; and
   - Audit program.

2.   Determine the extent to which the board and senior management is involved in risk control and monitoring systems. Consider

   - Types and frequency of board and senior management reviews used to determine adherence to policies, operating procedures, and strategic initiatives, including those related to functionally regulated entities;

   - The adequacy, timeliness, and distribution of management information reports;

   - The board's and senior management's responsiveness to risk control deficiencies and the effectiveness of their corrective action and follow-up activities; and

   - Quality and effectiveness of the annual account review process.

3.   Evaluate the adequacy and effectiveness of risk assessment processes and models and how such processes are used to control and monitor risk. Consider whether management uses processes such as

   - Performance attribution analysis,
   - Portfolio stress testing,

- Back testing, and
- Model validation processes.

4. If the bank has a separate risk management function for investment management, review its purpose, structure, reporting process, and effectiveness. Consider the following:

- Size, complexity, strategic plans, and trends in investment management services activities;

- Independence and objectivity;

- Quality and quantity of personnel; and

- Quality of risk assessment, transaction testing, monitoring systems, and reporting processes.

5. Evaluate the investment management compliance program. Consider the following:

- Extent of board and senior management commitment and support;

- Line management responsibility and accountability;

- Formalization, transaction testing, reporting structures, and follow-up processes;

- Qualifications and performance of compliance officer and supporting personnel;

- Communication systems; and

- Training programs.

6. If the bank has implemented a control self-assessment program, obtain information on its assessment of controls in investment management services. Evaluate the program and the results of recent control self-assessments of investment management lines of business and support functions.

7.   Review the bank's audit program for investment management services. A key goal of this review is to determine how much reliance can be placed on internal and external audit work. In the course of the review,

- Select and complete appropriate examination procedures from the "Internal and External Audits" booklet of the *Comptroller's Handbook*. Coordinate the selection of procedures with the examiner responsible for evaluating the bank's audit program.

- Obtain appropriate internal audit reports, work papers, and follow-up reports, including audit activity on functionally regulated subsidiaries and affiliates. Disseminate the reports to the appropriate examiners for review and follow-up.

- Determine the adequacy and effectiveness of the internal audit program relating to investment management by reviewing

   - The independence, qualifications, and competency of audit staff;
   - The timing, scope, and results of audit activity; and
   - The quality of audit reports, work papers, and follow-up processes.

- If the review of audit reports and work papers raises questions about audit effectiveness, discuss the issues with appropriate examiners and determine whether the scope of the audit review should be expanded. Issues that might require an expanded scope include

   - Unexplained or unexpected changes in auditors or significant changes in the audit program;
   - Inadequate scope of the investment management audit program;
   - Audit work papers that are deficient or do not support audit conclusions;
   - High-growth areas in investment management that lack adequate audit coverage; and
   - Inappropriate actions by insiders to influence the findings or scope of audits.

- Draw conclusions about the adequacy and effectiveness of the investment management audit program and forward the findings and recommendations, if applicable, to the examiner responsible for evaluating the bank's audit program.

Conclusions

Objective: To consolidate the conclusions and recommendations from the various investment management examination activities into final conclusions on the quantity of risk and quality of risk management.

1. Obtain conclusion memoranda and other risk assessment products from completed examination programs.

2. Discuss the individual examination findings with the responsible examiners and ensure that conclusions and recommendations are accurate, supported, and appropriately communicated.

3. Determine and document the recommended rating for asset management based on the factors listed in the Uniform Interagency Trust Rating System (UITRS.)

4. Finalize investment management services risk and risk management conclusions for input into the following, where applicable:

   ☐ Core knowledge database
   ☐ Core assessment standards (CAS)
   ☐ Risk assessment system (RAS)
   ☐ UITRS
   ☐ CAMELS
   ☐ Report of examination
   ☐ Asset management profile (AMP)

Objective: To communicate examination findings and initiate corrective action, if applicable.

1. Provide the EIC the following information, when applicable:

   • Conclusions on the impact of investment management on the applicable CAS, including the CAMELS and internal controls sections.

   • Conclusions on the impact of investment management on the applicable RAS factors.

- UITRS ratings recommendations.

- Draft report of examination comments.

- Matters requiring attention (MRA).

- Violations of law and regulation.

- Other recommendations provided to bank management.

2.   Discuss examination findings with the EIC and adjust findings and recommendations as needed. If the fiduciary asset management rating is 3 or worse, or the level of any risk factor is moderate and increasing or high because of asset management activities, contact the supervisory office before conducting the exit meeting with management.

3.   Hold an exit meeting with appropriate investment management committees and/or other risk managers to communicate examination conclusions and obtain commitments for corrective action, if applicable. Allow management time before the meeting to review draft examination conclusions and report comments.

4.   Prepare final comments for the report of examination as requested by the EIC. Perform a final check to determine whether comments

- Meet OCC report of examination guidelines.

- Support assigned UITRS ratings.

- Contain accurate violation citations.

5.   If there are MRA comments, enter them in the OCC's electronic information system. Ensure that the comments are consistent with MRA content requirements.

6.   Prepare appropriate comments for the fiduciary examination conclusion memorandum. Supplement the memorandum's comments, when appropriate, to include the following:

- The objectives and scope of completed supervisory activities;

- Reasons for changes in the supervisory strategy, if applicable;

- Overall conclusions, recommendations for corrective action, and management commitments and time frames; and

- Comments on any recommended administrative actions, enforcement actions, and civil money penalty referrals.

7. Update applicable sections of the electronic file, including:

- UITRS ratings,

- RAS (if requested by the bank EIC),

- Violations of law or regulation, and the

- Core knowledge database.

8. Prepare a recommended supervisory strategy for the subsequent supervisory cycle and provide it to the asset management EIC for review and approval.

9. Prepare a memorandum or update work programs with any information that will facilitate future examinations.

10. Organize and reference work papers in accordance with OCC guidelines.

11. Complete and distribute assignment evaluations for assisting examiners.

General Procedures — Registered Investment Advisers

The following procedures are to be used during a risk assessment of a national bank's registered investment adviser (RIA) subsidiary or holding company affiliate if such affiliate provides investment management services to the bank. The purpose of the risk assessment is to identify and estimate the types and level of risks posed to the bank by the activities of the RIA and to determine compliance with applicable legal requirements under the OCC's jurisdiction. The review will normally be based on supervisory information obtained during routine meetings with bank risk managers or during regularly scheduled monitoring of bank information reports.

If the risk assessment identifies potential material risks to the bank from the RIA's activities, the OCC may seek additional information or reports from the appropriate functional regulator. If such information or report is insufficient or not made available, the OCC may seek to obtain it from the RIA only if the information or report is necessary to assess

- A material risk to the affiliated national bank,

- Compliance with a federal law the OCC has specific jurisdiction to enforce with respect to the RIA, or

- The system for monitoring and controlling operational and financial risks that may pose a threat to the safety and soundness of the affiliated national bank.

These limitations do not restrict the OCC from seeking information on functionally regulated activities conducted directly by the bank, nor from seeking information on an RIA from the bank or sources other than the RIA.

Similar limitations apply to the direct examination of the registered adviser. The OCC may directly examine the registered adviser only when:

- There is reasonable cause to believe that the company is engaged in activities that pose a material risk to the affiliated national bank;

- After reviewing relevant reports, a reasonable determination is made that an examination of the company is necessary to adequately inform the OCC of the system for monitoring and controlling operational and financial risks that may pose a threat to the safety and soundness of the affiliated national bank; or

- Based on reports and other information available, there is reasonable cause to believe that the company is not in compliance with federal law that the OCC has specific jurisdiction to enforce against the company, including provisions relating to transactions with affiliates, and the national bank.

These limitations do not apply when the functionally regulated activity is conducted directly by the bank. In that case, the functional regulator is responsible for interpreting and enforcing laws under its jurisdiction and the activity is also subject to OCC supervision for safety and soundness reasons or based on separate statutory authority.

Before an examiner requests information from or conducts an examination of a functionally regulated entity, the following information should be discussed with the appropriate deputy comptroller:

- The identity of the functional regulator and the name, address, and telephone number of a primary contact at the functional regulator (if applicable); and

- A detailed description of the information to be requested or reason(s) for requesting the information or for conducting the examination activity consistent with GLBA requirements, as set forth in OCC Memorandum 00-1, plus a hard copy of the proposed request to be delivered to the functional regulator.

Objective: To perform a preliminary risk assessment of the types and level of risks posed to the bank by an RIA subsidiary or affiliate.

1. If appropriate and relevant, obtain the following information and reports applicable to the RIA from the bank:

    ❑ Board of director's minutes and information reports.
    ❑ Oversight committee's minutes and information reports.
    ❑ Strategic plans and fiscal and interim financial reports.
    ❑ Risk management information reports.
    ❑ Compliance and audit program reports.
    ❑ Policies and procedures used by the bank to oversee the RIA.
    ❑ Litigation reports.
    ❑ Client complaint files.

2. Discuss the following with the bank's risk managers:

    • Significant risk issues and management strategies relating to the RIA.
    • Significant changes in strategies, services, and distribution channels.
    • Significant changes in organization, policies, controls, and information systems.
    • External factors affecting the RIA and strategies to address these issues.

3. Complete the preliminary risk assessment of the bank, and discuss it with the EICs for asset management and the bank for perspective and strategy coordination. Consider the following:

    • The adviser's strategic plan and its impact on the bank;
    • The significance of current and planned revenue from the adviser in relation to bank revenue;
    • The amount of capital provided to and consumed by the adviser;
    • The impact on the bank's liquidity from providing resources to the adviser either through direct funding or from reputation risk; and
    • The adviser's and the bank's systems for monitoring revenue sensitivity to changing market conditions.

Objective: Establish the objectives, scope and work plans for the supervisory review of risk posed to the bank by the activities of the RIA to be completed during the bank's supervisory cycle.

1.   Based on the preliminary risk assessment, and in consultation with the bank EIC, the asset management EIC, and other appropriate regulatory agencies, prepare and submit a final review planning memorandum for approval by the bank's EIC that includes the following information:

- A preliminary business and risk assessment profile of the RIA. Refer to the "Asset Management" booklet for guidance.

- The review's objectives.

- The review's timing and projected workdays.

- The review's scope. The scope should be consistent with the preliminary risk assessment and focus on the identification and estimation of risk posed to the bank by the RIA's activities. Examples of higher risk activities include advising or managing portfolios with the following types of investments:

    - Proprietary investment products;
    - Alternative investments such as private equity funds, hedge funds, and structured investment products;
    - Closely held businesses and real estate; and
    - Large asset concentrations, including own bank stock.

- Required examiner resources to complete the review.

- The types of bank communication planned, such as meetings and final written products.

2.   Complete the following activities after the EIC has approved the planning memorandum:

- Select the asset management staff and make assignments consistent with the objectives, scope, and time frames of the planned review.

- Discuss the review plan with appropriate bank personnel and make suitable arrangements for on-site bank accommodations and additional information requests.

- Contact each member of the review team and provide necessary details concerning schedules and assignment responsibilities.

- These procedures should be completed in close consultation with and with authorization from the bank EIC and the asset management EIC.

If necessary, refer to the "Examination Planning and Control," "Large Bank Supervision," and "Asset Management" booklets of the *Comptroller's Handbook* for additional information on planning supervisory activities.

Quantity of Risk — Registered Investment Advisers

Conclusion: The RIA (does/does not) pose material risks to the bank.

Transaction Risk

Conclusion: The quantity of transaction risk posed to the bank by the RIA is (low, moderate, high).

Objective: To identify and estimate the quantity of transaction risk posed to the bank from the RIA's business activities.

1. Analyze bank-obtained information reports relating to transaction processing and information reporting in the RIA. Consider the following structural factors:

   - The volume, type, and complexity of bank transactions, products, and services offered through the RIA;
   - The condition, security, capacity, and recoverability of systems;
   - The complexity and volume of conversions, integrations, and system changes;
   - The development of new markets, products, services, technology, and delivery systems to maintain competitive position and gain strategic advantage; and
   - The volume and severity of bank operational, administrative, and accounting control exceptions and losses from fraud and operating errors relating to the RIA.

2. Analyze and discuss with appropriate risk managers at the bank how the following factors affect the quantity of transaction risk related to the RIA:

   - The impact of strategic factors, including marketing plans and the development of new markets, products, services, technology, and delivery systems;
   - The impact of acquisition and divestiture strategies; and
   - The maintenance of an appropriate balance between technology innovation and secure operations.

3. Analyze and discuss with appropriate risk managers at the bank how the following factors affect the quantity of transaction risk related to the RIA:

    - The impact of external factors including economic, industry, competitive, and market conditions; legislative and regulatory changes; and technological advancement;
    - The impact of infrastructure threats on the bank's ability to deliver timely support and service; and
    - The ability of service providers to provide and maintain service level performance that meets the 'requirements of the RIA.

4. Obtain the results of the bank information systems examination activities. Analyze and discuss the conclusions and recommendations with the assigned examiner(s) as they relate to the RIA.

5. Reach a conclusion on the quantity of transaction risk posed to the bank by the RIA's business activities.

Compliance Risk

Conclusion: The quantity of compliance risk posed to the bank by the RIA is (low, moderate, high).

Objective: To identify and estimate the quantity of compliance risk posed to the bank by the RIA's business activities.

1. Select a judgmental sample of fiduciary accounts in which the bank has investment discretion or provides investment advice for a fee, and has delegated investment authority for those accounts to the RIA.

2. Review each selected account for compliance with relevant investment management criteria established in:

   • The governing instrument or contract;
   • Federal, state, and local law and regulation;
   • The account's investment policy statement, if available;
   • Internal policies, procedures, and control processes; and
   • Contracts with third-party service providers.

3. Obtain and analyze the type and level of policy exceptions, internal control deficiencies, and law violations that have been identified and reported internally by the bank. Review information from the following sources:

   ❑ Board's and committee's minutes and reports.
   ❑ Risk management division's reports.
   ❑ Compliance reports.
   ❑ Control self-assessment reports.
   ❑ Internal and external audit reports.
   ❑ Regulatory reports.
   ❑ Other OCC examination programs.

4. Obtain and analyze the type and volume of bank litigation and consumer complaints related to the RIA.

5. Discuss significant litigation and complaints with the appropriate bank risk managers, and determine the risk to capital and the

appropriateness of corrective action and follow-up processes. If necessary, refer to the "Litigation and Other Legal Matters" booklet of the *Comptroller's Handbook* for additional procedures.

6.   Reach a conclusion on the quantity of compliance risk posed to the bank by the RIA's business activities. If applicable, consider the following core assessment factors:

   - The nature and extent of business activities, including new products and services;

   - The volume and significance of noncompliance and nonconformance with policies and procedures, laws, regulations, prescribed practices, and ethical standards; and

   - The amount and significance of litigation and customer complaints.

Strategic Risk

Conclusion: Aggregate strategic risk posed to the bank by the RIA is (low, moderate, high).

Objective: To identify and estimate strategic risk posed to the bank by the RIA's business activities.

1. Analyze the RIA's strategic plan by considering the following strategic factors:

    •   The magnitude of change in established corporate mission, goals, culture, values, or risk tolerance;
    •   The financial objectives as they relate to the bank's short- and long-term goals;
    •   The market situation, including product, customer demographics, and geographic position;
    •   Diversification by product, geography, and customer demographics;
    •   Past performance in offering new products and services;
    •   Risk of implementing innovative or unproven products, services, or technologies;
    •   Merger and acquisition plans and opportunities; and
    •   Potential or planned entrance into new businesses, product lines, or delivery channels, or implementation of new systems.

2. Discuss the strategic plan with appropriate bank risk managers and assess the impact of the following external factors on strategic risk.

    •   Economic, industry, and market conditions (impact on projected revenue);
    •   Legislative and regulatory change;
    •   Technological advances; and
    •   Competition.

3. Analyze conclusions from the "Quality of Risk Management" procedures completed during the review. Incorporate those conclusions into the evaluation of strategic risk from the RIA's business activities. Also consider the following factors:

- The expertise of senior management and the effectiveness of the board of directors;
- The priority and compatibility of personnel, technology, and capital resources allocation with strategic initiatives;
- Past performance in offering new products or services and evaluating potential and consummated acquisitions;
- Performance in implementing new technology or systems;
- The effectiveness of management's methods of communicating, implementing, and modifying strategic plans, and consistency with stated risk tolerance;
- The adequacy and independence of controls to monitor business decisions;
- The responsiveness to identified deficiencies in internal controls; and
- The quality, integrity, timeliness, and relevance of reports to the board of directors necessary to oversee strategic decisions.

4. Reach a conclusion on the impact of the RIA's business activities on the bank's level of strategic risk.

Reputation Risk

Conclusion: Aggregate reputation risk to the bank from the RIA is (low, moderate, high).

Objective: To identify and estimate reputation risk posed to the bank by the RIA's business activities.

1. Discuss with appropriate bank risk managers the impact of the strategic factors listed below on reputation risk from the RIA:

    - The volume and types of assets and number of accounts under management or administration;
    - Merger and acquisition plans and opportunities; and
    - Potential or planned entrance into new businesses, product lines, or technologies (including new delivery channels), particularly those that may test legal boundaries.

2. Discuss with appropriate risk managers the impact of the factors listed below on reputation risk from the RIA:

    - The market's or public's perception of the corporate mission, culture, and risk tolerance of the bank and the RIA;
    - The market's or public's perception of the bank's and the RIA's financial stability;
    - The market's or public's perception of the quality of products and services offered by the bank and the RIA; and
    - The impact of economic, industry, and market conditions; legislative and regulatory change; technological advances; and competition.

3. Analyze conclusions from the "Quality of Risk Management" procedures completed during the review. Incorporate those conclusions into the evaluation reputation risk from the RIA's business activities. If applicable, consider the following factors:

    - Past performance in offering new products or services and in conducting due diligence prior to startup;

- Past performance in developing or implementing new technologies and systems;
- The nature and amount of litigation and customer complaints;
- The expertise of senior management and the effectiveness of the board of directors in maintaining an ethical, self-policing culture;
- Management's willingness and ability to adjust strategies based on regulatory changes, market disruptions, market or public perception, and legal losses;
- The quality and integrity of management information systems and the development of expanded or newly integrated systems;
- The adequacy and independence of controls used to monitor business decisions;
- The responsiveness to deficiencies in internal control;
- The ability to minimize exposure from litigation and customer complaints;
- The ability to communicate effectively with the market, public, and media;
- Policies, practices, and systems protecting information customers might consider private or confidential from deliberate or accidental disclosure; and
- Management's responsiveness to internal, external, and regulatory review findings.

4.   Reach a conclusion on the impact of the RIA's business activities on the bank's level of reputation risk.

Quality of Risk Management — Registered Investment Advisers

Conclusion: The quality of the bank's risk management over the RIA is (strong, satisfactory, weak).

Policies

Conclusion: The bank has adopted (strong, satisfactory, weak) risk management policies applicable to the RIA.

The following are the core assessment standards applicable to risk management policies that should be considered when completing these procedures:

- The consistency of policies with the bank's overall strategic direction and throughout the organization.
- The appropriateness of guidelines that establish risk limits or positions and whether periodic revaluation is required.
- The reasonableness of definitions that determine policy exceptions and guidelines for approving policy exceptions.
- The structure of the bank's operations and whether responsibility and accountability are assigned at every level.
- The periodic review and approval of policies by the board or an appropriate committee.
- The structure of the compliance operation and whether responsibility and accountability are assigned at every level.

Objective: To determine the adequacy and effectiveness of bank policies applicable to the RIA.

1. Identify and obtain bank policies related to the RIA, including those related to information systems.

2. Review policy documents and determine whether they

- Are formally approved by the board, or a designated committee(s);

- Effectively address the bank's relationship with the RIA and applicable law;

- Outline the bank's investment management goals and objectives, investment philosophy, fiduciary responsibilities, ethical culture, risk tolerance standards, and risk management framework that will be applied to the RIA;

- Address all significant products and services provided by the RIA to the bank including

  - The types and size of acceptable accounts,
  - A list and description of investment products and styles,
  - Compensation schedules,
  - Descriptions of marketing and distribution channels, and
  - How new products and services are developed and approved.

- Address the bank's organizational structure and supervisory framework for managing risk associated with the RIA by establishing

  - Organizational and functional charts;
  - Defined lines of authority and responsibility;
  - Delegation authority and approval processes;
  - Processes to select, employ, and evaluate legal counsel;
  - Standards for dealings with affiliated organizations; and
  - Personnel practices.

- Establish portfolio management processes for accounts managed by the RIA, if applicable, that include appropriate guidelines for

  - Reviewing and accepting accounts and performing periodic portfolio reviews,
  - Economic and capital market analyses and reporting,
  - The development and implementation of portfolio investment policy programs,
  - Portfolio trading and broker selection, and
  - Selecting and monitoring third-party service providers.

- Address bank information systems and technology applications for monitoring RIA activities such as

- Accounting and other transaction record keeping systems;
- Management information system requirements;
- Portfolio management software that provides valuation, performance analysis, simulation, and trading interface applications and abilities;
- Investment trading systems; and
- Systems security and disaster contingency plans.

- Establish appropriate bank information reporting and risk monitoring processes for accounts managed by the RIA, if applicable, that include

  - Internal investment performance and risk management reporting standards;
  - Policy exception tracking and reporting processes;
  - Client reporting guidelines;
  - Control self-assessment processes;
  - Portfolio stress-testing, back-testing, and model validation processes;
  - Customer complaint resolution procedures; and
  - Performance reviews of third-party service providers.

3. Evaluate the policy review process and determine whether changes in risk tolerance, strategic direction, products and services, or the external environment are adequately and effectively reviewed.

4. Through discussion with management and other examiners, identify parts of the policy requiring development or revision. Consider the following as they relate to bank usage of RIA products and services:

    - Recently developed and distributed products and services;
    - Discontinued products, services, organizational structures, and information systems; and
    - Recent updates or revisions of existing policies and procedures.

5. Draw a conclusion on the adequacy and effectiveness of the bank's risk management policies relating to the RIA.

Processes

Conclusion: The bank has (strong, satisfactory, weak) processes for managing risk posed by the RIA.

The following are the core assessment standards applicable to risk management processes that should be considered when completing these procedures:

- The adequacy of processes that communicate policies and expectations to appropriate personnel.
- The production of timely, accurate, complete, and relevant management information.
- The adequacy of processes and systems to approve, monitor, and report on compliance with policy.
- The appropriateness of the approval process for policy exceptions.
- The adequacy of internal control, including segregation of duties, dual control, and authority commensurate with duties.
- Management's responsiveness to regulatory, industry, and technology changes.
- The adequacy of processes defining the systems architecture for transaction processing and for delivering products and services.
- The effectiveness of processes developed to ensure the integrity and security of systems and the independence of operating staff.
- The adequacy of processes to ensure the reliability and retention of information (e.g., data creation, processing, storage, and delivery).
- The quality of physical and logical security to protect the confidentiality of customer and corporate information.
- The capabilities of the front and back office systems to support current and projected operations.
- The adequacy of corporate contingency plans and business resumption plans for relevant data centers, file servers, PCs, networks, service providers and business units.
- The adequacy of contracts and management's ability to monitor relationships with the RIA and other third-party vendors.
- The capacity to deliver timely services and to respond rapidly to normal service interruptions or to attacks and intrusions from external sources.

- Whether risk measurement systems are appropriate to the nature and complexity of activities, and how these systems are incorporated into the decision-making process.
- The adequacy of processes assimilating legislative and regulatory changes into all aspects of the company.
- The commitment to allocate appropriate resources to training and compliance.
- The extent to which violations or noncompliance are identified internally and corrected.
- The adequacy of integrating compliance considerations into all phases of corporate planning, including the development of new products and services.

Objective: To determine the adequacy and effectiveness of supervision by the bank's board and senior management.

1.   Determine how supervisory oversight of the RIA is organized and whether clear lines of authority, responsibility, and accountability are established through all levels of the organization. Obtain and evaluate the following:

- Bank bylaws and resolutions.
- Strategic plan and business strategies, including those related to functionally regulated entities.
- Board and management committees, charters, minutes, and reports.
- Management structures, authorities, and responsibilities.
- Other organizational structures.

2.   If the board has delegated RIA supervisory oversight to one or more committees, review each committee's composition, charter, meeting frequency, attendance, information reports, and board reporting processes for consistency with board guidance and regulatory requirements.

3   Evaluate the bank's strategic planning process for the RIA. This procedure generally applies to the bank's subsidiary RIA. Consider the following questions:

- Does the process require the formulation and adoption of a long-term strategic plan supported by short-term business plans?

- Is the RIA's strategic planning process part of the bank's overall strategic and financial planning processes?

- Does the bank's process require periodic assessment, updating, and re-affirmations of the RIA's strategic plans?

- Does the bank's process consider significant factors that affect the RIA, such as internal risk tolerance standards, the corporate ethical culture, available financial resources, management expertise, technology capabilities, operating systems, competition, economic and market conditions, and legal and regulatory issues?

- Does the bank's planning process relating to the RIA evaluate and determine the amount of capital necessary to support the business?

- Does the bank's planning process include an effective means of communicating strategies, financial performance goals, and risk tolerance standards to the RIA?

4. Evaluate bank management processes for monitoring how the RIA implements the strategic plan and reports performance to the bank's board or the designated oversight body. Consider the following:

- Are policies and procedures consistent with the bank's strategic plan and policy guidelines?

- Are the development, implementation, and monitoring of short-term business plans consistent with board-established planning processes?

- Does the bank's board, or its designated oversight body, receive reports from the RIA that provide accurate, reliable, understandable, and relevant information about the following:

  - Success in meeting strategic goals and objectives;

  - Quantity and direction of investment management risks;

  - Adequacy of risk management systems;

        – Financial performance analyses, including the adequacy of capital allocated to the business; and

        – Summaries of changes to risk and business strategies, corrective actions, and proposed recommendations to address excessive risk levels or remedy control weaknesses.

5. Reach a conclusion on the quality of the bank's supervisory oversight of the RIA.

Objective: To determine the adequacy and effectiveness of third-party service provider selection and monitoring processes.

1. Evaluate bank policies and processes for reviewing the selection and monitoring of third-party service providers used by the bank's affiliated RIA. Discuss the policies and processes with appropriate bank risk managers. Document significant weaknesses in risk management processes. Consider the following in reaching conclusions:

   - The quality of the due diligence review process;
   - The contract negotiation and approval process;
   - Risk assessment processes;
   - Risk management and audit division participation;
   - Vendor monitoring processes, such as the assignment of responsibility, the frequency of reviews, and the quality of information reports reviewed; and
   - How well the vendor resolves problems.

Personnel

Conclusion: The bank has (strong, satisfactory, weak) personnel managing risk posed to the bank by the RIA.

The following are the core assessment standards applicable to personnel that should be considered when completing these procedures:

- The depth of technical and managerial expertise.

- The appropriateness of performance management and compensation programs.
- The appropriateness of management's response to identified deficiencies in policies, processes, personnel, and control systems.
- The level of turnover of critical staff.
- The adequacy of training.
- The ability of managers to implement new products, services, and systems in response to changing business, economic, or competitive conditions.
- The understanding of and adherence to the strategic direction and risk tolerance as defined by senior management and the board.

Objective: To determine the adequacy of the bank's evaluation of the RIA's management and supporting personnel.

1. Review the bank's process for evaluating the experience, education, and other training of the RIA's management and key supporting personnel. The bank's personnel review should include portfolio managers, research analysts, traders, business line managers, and other personnel who manage risk within the RIA.

2. Determine whether the bank's review assesses the adequacy of the RIA's personnel by considering the following:

   - The types and complexity of clients and the investment advisory services provided;
   - The RIA's compatibility with the bank's investment management services and corporate strategic initiatives,
   - The types and complexity of information processing and reporting systems; and
   - Knowledge of the bank's investment management policies and code of ethics, if applicable.

3. Review recent RIA staffing analyses plans that are available from the bank. Evaluate the bank's determination regarding the adequacy of the RIA's staffing level. Determine whether it considers

   - Current strategic initiatives and financial goals;
   - Current business volume, complexity, and risk profile;
   - The impact of company-initiated cost-cutting programs, if applicable;

- Success in hiring and retaining high-quality personnel;
- Level and trends of staff turnover, particularly in key positions;
- The quality and reasonableness of management succession plans; and
- The quality of training programs.

4. Assess the quality of bank personnel responsible for monitoring risk with the RIA. Determine whether

- Lines of authority and individual duties and responsibilities are clearly defined and communicated.

- Personnel are qualified and adequately trained for their positions and responsibilities.

- Personnel perform tasks outside their job descriptions that lower their overall performance or increase risk to the bank.

Control Systems

Conclusion: The bank has (strong, satisfactory, weak) control systems for managing risk posed by the RIA.

The following are the core assessment standards applicable to risk management control systems that should be considered when completing these procedures:

- The timeliness, accuracy, completeness, and relevance of management information systems, reports, monitoring, and control functions.
- The scope, frequency, effectiveness, and independence of the risk review, quality assurance, and internal/external audit functions.
- The effectiveness of exception monitoring systems that identify, measure, and track incremental risk exposure by how much (in frequency and amount) the exceptions deviate from policy and established limits, and corrective actions.
- The independent testing of processes to ensure ongoing reliability and integrity (e.g., Internet penetration testing).
- The adequacy of systems to monitor capacity and performance.

- The adequacy of controls over new product and systems development.
- The independent use and validation of measurement tools.

Objective: To determine the adequacy and effectiveness of the bank's control and monitoring systems relating to the RIA.

1. Determine and evaluate the types of control and monitoring systems used by the bank's board and senior management. Consider the following:

    - Board and senior management risk monitoring processes,
    - Risk management groups,
    - Committee structures and responsibilities,
    - Management information systems,
    - Quantitative risk measurement systems,
    - Compliance programs,
    - Control self-assessment processes, and
    - Audit program.

2. Determine the extent to which the bank's board and senior management is involved in supervising the RIA's business activities. Consider

    - Types and frequency of board and senior management reviews used to determine adherence to policies, operating procedures, and strategic initiatives, including those related to functionally regulated entities;
    - The adequacy, timeliness, and distribution of management information reports; and
    - The board's and senior management's responsiveness to risk control deficiencies and the effectiveness of their corrective action and follow-up activities.

3. If the bank has a separate risk management function responsible for the RIA, review its purpose, structure, reporting process, and effectiveness. Consider the following:

    - Size, complexity, strategic plans, and trends in investment management services activities;
    - Independence and objectivity;
    - Quality and quantity of personnel; and

- Quality of risk assessment, transaction testing, monitoring systems, and reporting processes.

4. Review the bank's assessment of the RIA's compliance program. Consider the following:

    - Extent of board and senior management commitment and support;
    - Line management responsibility and accountability;
    - Formalization, transaction testing, reporting structures, and follow-up processes;
    - Qualifications and performance of compliance officer and supporting personnel;
    - Communication systems; and
    - Training programs.

6. If the bank has implemented a control self-assessment program, obtain information on the control self-assessments performed by the RIA. Evaluate the results of control self-assessments completed by the RIA.

7. Obtain internal and external audit reports and follow-up reports pertaining to the RIA completed since the previous supervisory review:

    - Determine the adequacy and effectiveness of the internal and external audit work on the RIA by considering the following:

        - The independence, qualifications, and competency of audit staff;
        - The timing, scope, and results of audit activity; and
        - The quality of audit reports, work papers (if reviewed), and follow-up processes.

    - If the review of audit reports and work papers raises questions about audit effectiveness, discuss the issues with appropriate examiners and determine whether the scope of the audit review should be expanded. Issues that might require an expanded scope include

        - Unexplained or unexpected changes in auditors or significant changes in the audit program,
        - Inadequate scope of the investment management audit program,
        - Audit work papers that are deficient or do not support audit conclusions,

As of May 17, 2012, this guidance applies to federal savings associations in addition to national banks.*

- High-growth areas in investment management that lack adequate audit coverage, and
- Inappropriate actions by insiders to influence the findings or scope of audits.

- Draw conclusions about the adequacy and effectiveness of the bank's RIA audit program and forward the findings and recommendations, if applicable, to the examiner responsible for evaluating the bank's overall audit program.

Conclusions — Registered Investment Advisers

Objective: To consolidate and communicate the findings of the RIA review and initiate corrective action, if applicable.

1. Prepare a summary document that includes the following information, if applicable:

    *   Conclusions on the types and level of risk posed to the bank by the RIA's business activities.

    *   Conclusions on the impact of the RIA on the bank's core assessment and applicable risk assessment factors. Conclusions should address

        –   The effectiveness of the bank's system for monitoring and controlling operational and financial risks that may pose a threat to the safety and soundness of the bank; and

        –   Compliance with federal law that the OCC has specific jurisdiction to enforce with respect to the RIA.

    *   Other findings and recommendations for bank management.

    *   Whether the RIA should be examined. The OCC may examine a RIA only when:

        –   The OCC has reasonable cause to believe that the company is engaged in activities that pose a material risk to the national bank;

        –   The OCC reasonably determined, after reviewing relevant reports, that examination of the company is necessary to adequately inform the OCC of the system for monitoring and controlling operational and financial risks that may pose a threat to the safety and soundness of the national bank; or

        –   The OCC, based on reports and other available information, has reasonable cause to believe that the company is not in compliance with federal law that the OCC has specific jurisdiction to enforce against that company, including provisions relating to transactions with affiliates, and the OCC cannot make such determination through examination of the national bank.

2. Discuss the review's findings with the bank and asset management EICs and adjust findings and recommendations as needed. Decisions relating to an examination of the RIA should be made only after consultations with and the approval of the appropriate supervisory office authority.

3. Hold a meeting with appropriate bank oversight committees or the appropriate risk managers to communicate the review's conclusions and recommendations, if appropriate and if authorized by the bank EIC. Allow management time before the meeting for preliminary examination conclusions and draft report comments.

4. Prepare appropriate comments for the memorandum containing the fiduciary examination's conclusions. Supplement the memorandum, when appropriate, to include the following:

    - The objectives and scope of completed supervisory activities;

    - Reasons for changes in the supervisory strategy, if applicable;

    - Overall conclusions, recommendations for corrective action, and management commitments and time frames; and

    - Comments on recommended administrative actions, enforcement actions, and civil money penalty referrals, if applicable.

5. Prepare final comments for the bank report of examination as requested by the EIC. Perform a final check to determine whether comments

    - Meet OCC guidelines for reports of examination,
    - Support the review's conclusions and recommendations, and
    - Contain accurate violation citations.

6. If there are MRA comments, enter them in the OCC's electronic information system. Ensure that the comments are consistent with MRA content requirements.

7. Update applicable sections of the electronic file, including

    - UITRS ratings,
    - RAS (if requested by the bank EIC),
    - Violations of law or regulation, and the
    - Core knowledge database.

8. Prepare a recommended supervisory strategy for the subsequent supervisory cycle, and give it to the asset management EIC for review and approval.

9. Prepare a memorandum or update work programs with any information that will facilitate future examinations.

10. Organize and reference work papers in accordance with OCC guidelines.

11. Complete and distribute assignment evaluations for assisting examiners.

Appendix A: Portfolio Management Processes

This section discusses the processes that a fiduciary investment manager may follow to achieve the objectives of an account and effectively manage risk in an investment portfolio. For most fiduciaries, the legal requirements for prudent investment management require investment managers to follow the course of action of an informed investor. The fiduciary duty of caution does not require an investment manager to avoid risk, only to manage it prudently. The courts will judge a fiduciary on the process he or she used to manage a portfolio, not necessarily the investments' results.

The portfolio management process is virtually the same for all types of portfolios, regardless of size or purpose. While a formally structured and disciplined investment management process does not guarantee investment success, it does significantly increase the likelihood of maintaining a portfolio that withstands the test of private and public scrutiny and fiduciary standards of loyalty and prudence. For any portfolio management process to be effective, it must be a continual process that is responsive to changes in client needs and characteristics and capital market conditions.

The following guidelines present standardized, but flexible, processes in three broad and sometimes overlapping stages: investment policy development, implementation, and monitoring. The guidelines incorporate modern portfolio theory and elements of prudent fiduciary conduct. They reflect portfolio management techniques developed and followed by the professional investment management industry and incorporate legal elements of fiduciary conduct established by the Prudent Investor Rule and ERISA.

Stage 1 — Development of Investment Policy

The development of an appropriate and realistic investment policy is critical to the long-term success of any portfolio. The development of an investment policy consists of analyzing the investment assignment, identifying investment objectives, developing asset allocation guidelines, and establishing appropriate performance benchmarks, and culminates with the creation of an investment policy statement.

The Investment Assignment

The fiduciary should examine the governing instrument (trust or agency agreement) and understand its purpose, intent, investment directives, and granted investment authority and powers. It is important that all parties understand the purpose and intent of the document creating the fiduciary relationship. A fiduciary's investment responsibilities should be clearly established and documented. These actions will help the fiduciary develop a better investment policy and can limit future problems.

The fiduciary should develop an understanding of the characteristics and investment needs of the account's principals and beneficiaries. This may require reviewing each party's entire financial profile, if possible, to determine the portfolio's relationship to his or her other assets and income sources.

The fiduciary should evaluate the portfolio's current investment holdings to determine whether they are appropriate based on the account's purpose and investment needs. It is also prudent to analyze how others managed the portfolio and the recent investment performance of the portfolio.

Investment Objectives

After reviewing the governing document and account principals and beneficiaries, the fiduciary can identify and document the account's investment objectives. Investment objectives should

- Articulate the account's risk tolerance;

- Establish investment goals and return requirements; and

- Detail legal, liquidity, time horizon, taxes, and other special circumstances of the account, its principals, and beneficiaries.

Investment objectives should be a list of quantifiable investment results that are expected over a specified time frame. Objectives can be set for the total portfolio as well as for various asset categories and each individual investment, adviser, or fund. Objectives help to determine 1) which assets are allocated to the portfolio, 2) the portfolio's investment policy, and 3) how the portfolio's performance is evaluated and monitored.

A portfolio's investment objectives must make sense from the client's tax and legal standpoint. A portfolio's assets must be viewed together with the client's other assets, if possible, and blended with rational capital market expectations. In taxable accounts, return goals should be expressed in after-tax terms. When developing investment objectives for persons, remember the wealth accumulation life cycle and understand its effect on the investor's needs and constraints.

Asset Allocation Guidelines

Once an account's investment objectives have been established, the fiduciary manager must decide how to efficiently allocate portfolio assets among the various investment opportunities. Asset allocation decisions may be the most important decisions the fiduciary manager makes in terms of a portfolio's long-term investment performance. Asset allocation guidelines establish the type and amount of assets to be held under normal conditions and the average level of risk tolerance over the expected life of the portfolio. The guidelines must conform to investment constraints imposed by a client. For example, one account may permit only equity investments, another may impose restrictions on the use of financial derivatives, and still another may prohibit investing in a certain type of industry or country.

Asset allocation involves dividing the investment portfolio among asset markets, or categories of assets, to achieve appropriate diversification or a combination of expected return and risk consistent with the portfolio's objectives and risk tolerance. The types of assets traditionally allocated by banks include publicly traded equity and debt securities, and their cash equivalents. An increasing number of alternative investments have become accepted and used by both institutional and personal investors. Some examples include real estate, private equity funds, hedge funds, managed futures, commodities, and mineral interests.

The primary types of assets are often broken down into sectors and investment styles. Sectors can be differentiated by industry, country, market, and other social and economic characteristics. Some examples of investment styles are active, passive, growth, value, large capitalization, and small capitalization.

The concepts of modern portfolio theory and efficient frontiers can be applied to the problem of deciding how to allocate portfolio assets among the major asset categories. For example, allocations can be established using mean-variance quadratic computer programs that mathematically determine efficient portfolio mixes for different risk levels. The basic inputs are expected return, expected yields, risk estimates, and correlations (or covariances) for each asset category included in the analysis. Other inputs may include constraints such as target concentration limits of individual or group asset types and yield constraints on part, or all, of the portfolio.

The computer program determines the portfolio's expected return, variance, and standard deviation for different allocations of funds between the asset categories, and establishes the efficient set of portfolios, or optimal portfolios. The program can also develop portfolios based on the probability that an expected return will not be achieved, and can also be applied to multiple scenarios with probability forecasting. While asset allocation computer programs are useful and highly efficient for certain kinds of investment strategies, their effectiveness depends on the quality of modeling input and the knowledge, expertise, and judgment of the user.

Tax-exempt portfolios have been the focus of most asset allocation modeling programs. Personal investors are now requiring tax-aware asset allocation planning in order to minimize taxes and develop strategies that enhance estate planning structures. To be competitive, a bank will need asset allocation tools that can be efficiently applied to taxable portfolios.

A bank does not need to develop and maintain its own sophisticated asset allocation programming and computer capability. There are a variety of companies that provide quantitative asset allocation services.

Performance Benchmarks

From the asset allocation guidelines, an appropriate performance benchmark can be selected as a passive representation of a portfolio's investment objectives, strategy, and style. Performance benchmarks are used to make risk and return comparisons. Useful and effective benchmarks are:

- **Unambiguous**. The names and weights of investments comprising the benchmark are clearly delineated.

- **Investable**. The option is available to forego active management and simply hold the benchmark.

- **Measurable**. The benchmark's return can be readily determined on a reasonably frequent basis.

- **Appropriate**. The benchmark is consistent with the portfolio's investment strategy or the portfolio manager's investment style or biases.

- **Reflective of current investment opinions**. The manager has current investment knowledge of the benchmark.

- **Specified in advance**. The benchmark is constructed prior to the start of the performance evaluation period.

Selecting an appropriate benchmark is not an easy task, particularly for accounts with many different asset categories and beneficiaries. Each type of asset, and even each sub-sector, may have its own separate benchmark. This process reinforces the importance of having a clearly written investment policy with specific goals and objectives to improve a manager's ability to establish appropriate performance benchmarks. Subsequent changes to selected benchmarks must be carefully considered and fully documented by the fiduciary manager.

The most commonly used benchmark is a market index, such as the S&P 500 or a corporate bond index. Market indexes are viewed as independent representations of the market and are publicly available. Market indexes can also be combined to reflect a specific portfolio strategy or asset allocation structure. Problems with market indexes include the following:

- The index may not accurately reflect a portfolio's strategy or style;
- Indexes implicitly assume cost-free transactions;
- Most indexes assume that income is reinvested; and
- Investors cannot invest in some market indexes.

The "normal portfolio" of a particular manager, fund, or account is a specially constructed portfolio that represents an investment strategy's neutral position and displays average market exposures over time. While this type of benchmark may provide greater insight into a portfolio's performance, its construction can be costly, is easily manipulated, requires ongoing maintenance, and may be difficult to explain to clients.

Whether a benchmark is a publicly available index or a customized product, the fiduciary manager must understand the mechanics behind its construction before effectively analyzing portfolio performance relative to the benchmark. Benchmarks facilitate both the assessment of active management skill and the efficient allocation of funds among managers within all asset categories of a portfolio. They are essential investment tools for fiduciary managers.

The Investment Policy Statement

The creation of an appropriate investment policy document, or statement, is the culmination of analyzing the investment assignment, identifying investment objectives, determining asset allocation guidelines, and establishing performance measurement benchmarks. The lack of an investment policy statement, or the existence of a poorly developed one, is a weakness in portfolio management risk control.

A properly constructed investment policy statement can ensure the continuity of the investment program and limits second-guessing of investment decisions. It may also limit the temptation to increase portfolio risk to take advantage of perceived short-term market trends. The length and explicitness of the policy statement depends on the type of client, and the policy statement should be customized for each client. Refer to appendix E for guidance on developing investment policy statements.

Stage 2 — Implementing Investment Policy

Once the investment policy has been developed, the fiduciary portfolio manager must implement the policy's investment strategies (according to its guidelines and limits) and assign operational responsibilities. Specific activities include

- Selecting investment managers and advisers, if this function is to be outsourced;

- Selecting and acquiring investments based on the asset allocation guidelines in the investment policy;

- Monitoring and re-balancing the portfolio according to the investment policy and asset allocation guidelines; and

- Reviewing risk management reporting information and providing appropriate risk managers with investment performance and compliance reports.

Investment managers, internal and external, are selected for each asset category and decisions are made concerning the amount of money placed with each manager. Refer to appendix F for guidance on selecting and monitoring third-party investment managers and advisers.

Within each asset category and associated sectors, decisions are made concerning the specific assets to purchase and the amount of money to be invested in each one. The organization normally maintains an approved list of individual securities in each asset category or sub-sector. This regularly updated list should provide portfolio managers with recommendations in the form of expected return and risk characteristics of the security, including sensitivity to various factors. Portfolio managers use the securities list to construct investment portfolios according to the asset allocation guidelines.

Portfolio monitoring and revision is a continual and complicated process that requires extensive analysis and sound judgment. Asset categories may become over- or under-weighted in relation to the asset allocation guidelines because the returns on individual asset categories will vary over time. Portfolio re-balancing involves restoring the portfolio to appropriate percentage allocation ranges. Re-balancing requires the portfolio manager to make critical decisions about the cost of trading versus the cost of not trading. Re-balancing, when completed in a disciplined and controlled manner, can enhance performance and ensure compliance with the investment policy.

Tactical asset allocation (TAA), or targeted, short-term changes in the asset mix or sectors, may have a place in the portfolio management process. It is a variation of market timing, albeit a highly quantitative form. TAA managers shift their portfolio between asset categories in hopes of exiting overvalued markets and concentrating on undervalued markets. TAA managers hope to extract alpha, or investment performance in excess of expected return, by examining the long-term fundamentals of entire asset categories.

TAA style differs slightly from firm to firm, but the market leaders all evaluate the relative current expense of buying future cash flows for different asset categories and sectors. TAA assumes that the client's objectives and risk tolerance stay constant, but that the market environment changes and inefficiencies exist. To control TAA, the investment policy's asset allocation guidelines should incorporate prudent ranges of permissible reallocations.

Portfolio managers review performance and risk measurement reports to evaluate their success in achieving the goals and objectives of the portfolios.

Their performance and compliance with investment policies and strategies should be demonstrated through reports to appropriate risk managers in the investment organization. This reporting process should be formalized and documented. The reports should supply the following information:

- Total return over relevant time periods.
- Total return breakdown and attribution.
- Comparisons to portfolio objectives and benchmarks.
- Risk-adjusted return comparisons over relevant time periods.
- Compliance with portfolio guidelines and client needs.

Stage 3 — Monitoring Investment Policy

An effective monitoring program will provide the fiduciary manager with information to evaluate the investment policy's strengths and weaknesses and to keep the investment strategy on track in achieving the client's goals and objectives. The fiduciary manager must establish and monitor performance measurement standards suitable for the client and the portfolio. An effective monitoring program includes the following:

- A formalized and documented account review process that includes an annual investment policy review to analyze performance and reaffirm or change the investment policy, including asset allocation guidelines.

- The maintenance of current and relevant client information.

- Appropriate communication with clients.

- Comprehensive risk management reports relating to investment performance, risk levels, and policy exception identification and follow-up.

- Interim reviews of adherence to asset allocation and individual security guidelines, and of performance relative to established benchmarks.

- Monitoring of global and domestic economic conditions, capital markets trends, political environments, regulatory climates, and other competitive factors.

Appendix B: Trust Investment Law

This section provides an overview of trust investment law and the development and application of the Prudent Investor Rule of the Restatement (Third) of Trusts (PIR) and the Uniform Prudent Investor Act (UPIA). Bank trustees should consult with qualified legal counsel to determine if and how the PIR, the UPIA, or other applicable trust laws apply to the bank's trust accounts.

The foundation of trust law defining prudent investment decisions by trustees was established in 1830 by the Massachusetts Supreme Court in *Harvard College v. Amory*. The Harvard College standard is commonly known as the Prudent Man Rule (PMR).

> **"All that can be required of a trustee to invest, is, that he shall conduct himself faithfully and exercise a sound discretion. He is to observe how men of prudence, discretion, and intelligence manage their own affairs, not in regard to speculation, but in regard to the permanent disposition of their funds, considering the probable income, as well as the probable safety of the capital to be invested."**

Over the next century, the philosophies of state legislatures and courts changed from favoring flexibility in trust investing to a desire for more certainty and conservatism. In the first half of the twentieth century, most states enacted lists of specific types of investments that trustees were permitted to make, and courts established a series of subrules on what was prudent and what was not. Although this original standard compares a trustee to his contemporaries, suggesting a flexible standard, state courts and legislatures progressively restricted the latitude of trustees' investment decisions by introducing "legal lists" and requiring trustees to assess the prudence of each individual investment in isolation. Thus the flexibility and discretion of *Harvard College v. Amory* gave way to rules and restrictions.

In 1942, the American Bankers Association (ABA) promulgated its Model Prudent Man Investment Statute, which slightly modified the PMR.

> **"In acquiring, investing, reinvesting, exchanging, retaining, selling, and managing property for the benefit of another, a fiduciary shall exercise the judgment and care under the circumstances then prevailing, which men of prudence, discretion, and intelligence exercise in the management of their own affairs, not in regard to speculation but in regard to the permanent disposition of their funds, considering the probable income as well as probable safety of their capital."**

Since then, a significant majority of states have amended their statutes in recognition of changes in the economy, financial theory, and widely accepted investment products and techniques employed by the professional investment management community. Many state legislatures eliminated the legal investment lists and replaced them with prudent investment standards similar to the PMR, now the Prudent Person Rule (PPR). In addition, Congress imposed a similar prudence standard for the administration of pension and employee benefit trusts in the Employee Retirement Income Security Act (ERISA) enacted in 1974.

The concept of prudence in the judicial opinions and legislation is essentially relational or comparative. It resembles in this respect the "reasonable person" rule of tort law. A prudent trustee behaves as other trustees similarly situated would behave. The standard is, therefore, objective rather than subjective. Almost all rules of trust law are default rules, that is, rules that the settler may alter or abrogate. Traditional trust law also allows the beneficiaries of the trust to excuse a trust's investment performance if all beneficiaries are capable and properly informed.

Of the standards to which a trustee must adhere, the most important are that it exercise care, skill, and caution, and manifest loyalty and impartiality. A trustee's compliance with these duties is judged as of the time an investment decision is made, and not with the benefit of hindsight or subsequent developments, nor on the outcome of his or her investment decisions.

Modern Portfolio Theory

Modern portfolio theory (MPT) is a variety of portfolio construction, asset valuation, and risk measurement concepts that rely on the application of statistical and quantitative techniques. Among the concepts and models associated with the MPT are Markowitz's portfolio theory, the capital asset pricing model, the arbitrage pricing theory, and the Black-Scholes option pricing model. MPT is widely employed by the professional investment management community because it provides insights and principles for determining the optimal allocation of wealth among available investments in the marketplace and offers a generally accepted methodology for systematically evaluating risk.

MPT reflects contemporary economic understanding of the portfolio management process. It embraces scientific methods of understanding risk and return relationships and the importance of portfolio diversification. It gives substance to the legal parameters of prudence by developing quantitative techniques to assist in evaluating volatility, suitability, investment productivity, and diversification. It focuses attention on both the purpose and reasoning behind an investment decision.

MPT has significantly influenced the evolution of the standard of care governing trustees as enunciated in ERISA, the PIR, and the UPIA. It has also influenced how the investment management community develops, implements, and monitors an investment strategy and, in turn, has influenced the evolution of the standard of prudence governing trustees. MPT offers the following conclusions:

- The investment strategy and its performance must be judged for the whole portfolio rather than for each particular investment component.

- It is portfolio risk, not the risk posed by individual securities, that determines suitability and diversification decisions.

- An investment manager should consider any market instrument or investment vehicle that can be used to manage portfolio risk.

- An investment manager does not eliminate any investment opportunities simply because an investor has certain attributes. Investor-specific attributes like tax status, time horizon, and risk tolerance merely tilt a portfolio toward or away from certain types of securities.

A major insight of MPT is that an investment strategy and its performance must be judged on the basis of the portfolio as a whole, rather than on the basis of each investment in isolation. It is the effect on total portfolio risk that determines the prudence of including an investment in a portfolio. An investment manager should consider all available investment opportunities that can be used to manage portfolio risk.

MPT assesses risk in terms of the interrelationships of investments within a portfolio and the relationship of an individual investment to the entire portfolio. A portfolio may be diversified by investments whose values react oppositely to the same factors or stimuli. Investments whose values move in the same direction in response to stimuli may diversify a portfolio if the scale of their reaction is markedly different. The risk of a portfolio is a function of the interrelationships of its component investments.

A fiduciary applying elements of MPT can use investments viewed as risky individually to assemble a portfolio that provides an acceptable level of risk. An investment that might appear too risky by itself might, in fact, enhance a portfolio because of its imperfect correlation with other portfolio investments and its effect on the overall risk and return characteristics of the portfolio. MPT suggests that such a portfolio may have a significantly higher expected return than a portfolio constructed based on the restrictive PPR, without increasing overall portfolio risk.

The Prudent Investor Rule

The incorporation of MPT into trust law was significantly advanced by the adoption of the Restatement (Third) of Trusts by the American Law Institute in May 1990. ERISA's statutory and regulatory standards for prudent investing, diversification, and delegation of pension plan fiduciaries are also reflected in the Restatement (Third). Specifically, section 227 of the Restatement (Third) recognizes an expansion of the fiduciary responsibilities of trustees and provides greater latitude in fulfilling such responsibilities.

The American Law Institute's restatements of trusts have been influential with lawyers, professional trustees, and the courts over the years as summaries of state laws and judicial decisions governing the conduct of trustees. It has greatly influenced the development of trust law in the United States. But the positions adopted by the Institute are only commentaries on the law, not the law itself, and depend on the willingness of courts to follow them.

The PIR articulates standards by which a trustee's conduct can be guided and judged. The standards are intended to be general and flexible enough to accommodate changes in knowledge and concepts in the financial world and to allow the prudent use of any investments or investment techniques that serve the individual purposes of any specific trust. The PIR has five major principles:

- Sound diversification is fundamental to risk management and is ordinarily required of trustees.

- Risk and return are so directly related that trustees have a duty to analyze and make conscious decisions concerning the levels of risk appropriate to the purposes, distribution requirements, and other circumstances of the trust.

- Trustees have a duty to avoid fees, transaction costs, and other expenses not justified by the needs and realistic objectives of the trust's investment strategy.

- A trustee's duty to be impartial toward all beneficiaries requires a trustee to balance investment returns between producing current income and promoting purchasing power.

- Trustees have a duty as well as the authority to delegate investment authority as a prudent investor would.

From the Restatement of the Law Third, Trusts

§ 227. General Standard of Prudent Investment

The trustee is under a duty to the beneficiaries to invest and manage the funds of the trust as a prudent investor would, in light of the purposes, terms, distribution requirements, and other circumstances of the trust.

(a)   This standard requires the exercise of reasonable care, skill, and caution, and is to be applied to investments not in isolation but in the context of the trust portfolio and as a part of an overall investment strategy, which should incorporate risk and return objectives reasonably suitable to the trust.

(b)   In making and implementing investment decisions, the trustee has a duty to diversify the investments of the trust unless, under the circumstances, it is prudent not to do so.

(c)   In addition, the trustee must:

(1)   conform to fundamental fiduciary duties of loyalty (§ 170) and impartiality (§ 183);

(2)   act with prudence in deciding whether and how to delegate authority and in the selection and supervision of agents (§ 171); and

---

(3)   incur only costs that are reasonable in amount and appropriate to the investment responsibilities of the trusteeship (§ 188).

(d)   The trustee's duties under this Section are subject to the rule of §228, dealing primarily with contrary investment provisions of a trust or statute.

A portfolio's structure must reflect how a trust instrument views producing income for life tenants in relation to building residual assets for the trust's remaindermen. In most states, the allocation between income and principal, and thus between life tenants and remaindermen, is set forth in the Uniform Principal and Income Act of 1931 and the Revised Uniform Principal and Income Act of 1962. Although these acts are default rules that may be modified by the trust instrument, the vast majority of trusts simply follow the statute. These standards do not give trustees unlimited discretion to reclassify receipts as either income or principal. And the PIR does not alter traditional trust accounting and its allocation of income to income beneficiaries and principal to remainder beneficiaries.

The Revised Uniform Principal and Income Act of 1997 gives a trustee the discretion to allocate receipts either to income or principal if needed to rebalance the interests of income and remainder beneficiaries and to carry out the purposes of the trust. This change was made to alleviate the tension between modern investing practices and the traditional ideas about what constitutes the return on a trust portfolio. The revised act, however, has been adopted in only thirteen states as of July 31, 2000. States are also free to modify uniform acts when they adopt them, and not all states have included this provision.

The PIR represents an evolution in the definition of prudence incorporating the generally accepted analytical framework of MPT. It was promulgated to ameliorate the impact of restrictive judicial interpretations of the PPR. The PIR follows the evolutionary trend established by ERISA's statutory and regulatory standards for prudent investing, diversification, and delegation. A trustee's prudence is to be judged as of the time an investment decision is made. The benefit of hindsight or consideration of developments that occurred after a decision to acquire, retain, or dispose of an investment was made are not permissible in assessing prudence.

By adopting the basic elements of MPT, the PIR brings the standards governing trustee investment decision-making processes in line with the generally accepted practices of the larger professional investment management community. It authorizes trustees to formulate and implement an investment strategy that embraces more investment asset classes than were permitted by the restrictive judicial interpretations of the PPR. It provides trustees with more discretion in determining the investments that should comprise a trust portfolio, and creates the expectation that trustees will consider the entire universe of investment opportunities and not ignore any type or class of investment in constructing a portfolio. The PIR emphasizes that no specific investments or investment techniques are prudent or imprudent per se.

The PIR requires that the standard of prudence must be applied to the portfolio as a whole, not just to each individual investment in the portfolio. A trustee is required to determine the prudence of an investment not in isolation, but in terms of its anticipated effect on the whole portfolio. Also, in the case of structured products or assets with unique risk and return properties, the PIR does not eliminate the need for the trustee to evaluate the investment separately. All risks unique to any investment being considered must be evaluated and understood by the trustee, and then applied in the context of the whole portfolio.

The PIR makes the duty to diversify trust investments part of the standard of care. It recognizes that a trustee must seek the lowest level of portfolio risk for a particular level of expected return, or the highest return commensurate with acceptable risk. This trade-off between risk and return is optimally achieved through portfolio diversification. A trustee is under a duty to minimize unsystematic risk (elements of risk that are unique to a particular investment but that can be largely eliminated through diversification), because theory holds that the market will not compensate the investor for taking such risk. PIR commentary endorses the use of pooled investment vehicles, such as mutual and collective investment funds, as a prudent means of achieving adequate diversification in a trust portfolio.

The PIR abrogates the older trust law that forbade trustees from delegating decision-making authority over investments. This follows the trend of ERISA, the Uniform Management of Institutional Funds Act, and the Uniform Trustees Powers Act in encouraging the delegation of investment responsibilities to specialists. The PIR requires a trustee who delegates to act prudently in selecting, instructing, and monitoring the performance of agents, including investment managers.

The trustee must act prudently in deciding whether, to whom, and in what manner to delegate fiduciary authority in the administration of a trust. The trustee should consider all relevant circumstances in connection with the delegation of investment functions, including the knowledge, skill, capabilities, and compensation of both the trustee and agent. Other circumstances to be considered include the size of the trust, the nature and complexity of the trust assets, and the particular goals of the investment strategy.

The trustee is under a duty to supervise any agents to whom investment responsibilities are delegated. Decisions of delegation are matters of the trustee's judgment and discretion, and are not to be controlled by a court except in cases of discretionary abuse. Such an abuse of discretion can involve an imprudent delegation of authority as well as an imprudent failure to delegate.

The PIR is intended for a trust only if it is consistent with the terms of a trust and state law. Generally, the terms of the trust will control. If a state has adopted the PIR, or permits a trust to adopt it, then the terms of the trust will dictate whether the PIR applies to its investment activity. The terms of the trust may expand or limit the provisions of the PIR. A trust's terms will control a trustee's investment authorities and duties, even if different from the PIR, so long as they do not conflict with the law. But absent contrary provisions, or silence, in the terms of the trust, the PIR will govern if a state has adopted it. As of December 1999, 38 states have adopted the PIR.

While the PIR addresses investment guidance for private trusts, it may be used as guidance for other types of fiduciaries. Courts and regulators who supervise other types of fiduciaries will probably turn to the PIR for guidance just as they looked to the previous Restatement in the day of the old PMR. Since a significant majority of states and the professional investment management community have embraced the PIR, it is reasonable to anticipate that the remaining states, by statute or judicial decision, will implement the precepts of the PIR in determining the nature and extent of a trustee's duty of prudence in trust investment management.

The PIR asserts that the duty of caution does not call for the total avoidance of risk by trustees, but rather for its "prudent management." The emphasis is on active risk management processes. Under the PIR, the trustee has an affirmative duty to assess the risk tolerance of the trust and its beneficiaries and actively manage the risk elements of its investment portfolio. No objective, general legal standard can be set for a degree of risk that is or is not prudent. The degree of risk permitted for a particular trust is ultimately a matter of interpretation and judgment. This requires that a trustee make reasonable efforts to ascertain the purposes of the trust and to understand the types of investments suitable to those purposes in light of all the relevant circumstances.

The Uniform Prudent Investor Act

In response to the PIR, the National Conference of Commissioners on Uniform State Laws (NCC) in 1994 promulgated the UPIA. The NCC's charter is to promote uniformity among the 50 states in certain areas of law. The UPIA was created as a mode to be used by the states to update and codify trust investment law. The UPIA reflects the influence of MPT and incorporates the knowledge and experience of the professional investment management community. The act draws upon the revised standards for prudent trust investment in the PIR.

The UPIA governs the investment responsibilities of trustees, but it may also provide guidance for other types of fiduciary investment managers. The UPIA has been adopted in full by a majority of the state legislatures. Many other states have revised their PPR to conform to certain aspects of the UPIA. There are only a handful of states that have not adopted either the PIR or the UPIA.

Uniform Prudent Investor Act

§ 1.   Prudent Investor Rule

(a)   Except as otherwise provided in subsection (b), a trustee who invests and manages trust assets owes a duty to the beneficiaries of the trust to comply with the prudent investor rule set forth in this Act.

(b)   The prudent investor rule, a default rule, may be expanded, restricted, eliminated, or otherwise altered by the provisions of a trust. A trustee is not liable to a beneficiary to the extent that the trustee acted in reasonable reliance on the provisions of the trust.

§ 2.   Standard of Care: Portfolio Strategy; Risk and Return Objectives

(a)   A trustee shall invest and manage trust assets as a prudent investor would, but considering the purposes, terms, distribution requirements, and other circumstances of the trust. In satisfying this standard, the trustee shall exercise reasonable care, skill, and caution.

(b)   A trustee's investment and management decisions respecting individual assets must be evaluated not in isolation but in the context of the trust portfolio as a whole and as a part of an overall investment strategy having risk and return objectives reasonably suited to the trust.

(c)   Among the circumstances that a trustee shall consider in investing and managing trust assets are such of the following as are relevant to the trust or its beneficiaries:

(1)   general economic conditions;

(2)   the possible effect of inflation or deflation;

(3)   the expected tax consequences of investment decisions or strategies;

(4)   the role that each investment or course of action plays within the overall trust portfolio, which may include financial assets, interests in closely held enterprises, tangible and intangible personal property, and real property;

(5)   the expected total return from income and the appreciation of capital;

(6)   other resources of the beneficiaries;

(7)   needs for liquidity, regularity of income, and preservation or appreciation of capital; and

(8)   an asset's special relationship or special value, if any, to the purposes of the trust or to one or more of the beneficiaries.

(d)   A trustee shall make a reasonable effort to verify facts relevant to the investment and management of trust assets.

(e)   A trustee may invest in any kind of property or type of investment consistent with the standards of the Act.

(f)   A trustee who has special skills or expertise, or is named trustee in reliance upon the trustee's representation that the trustee has special skills or expertise, has a duty to use those special skills or expertise.

§ 3.   Diversification

A trustee shall diversify the investments of the trust unless the trustee reasonably determines that, because of special circumstances, the purposes of the trust are better served without diversifying.

§ 4. Duties at Inception of Trusteeship.

Within a reasonable time after accepting a trusteeship or receiving trust assets, a trustee shall review the trust assets and make and implement decisions concerning the retention and disposition of assets, in order to bring the trust portfolio into compliance with the purposes, terms, distribution requirements, and other circumstances of the trust, and with the requirements of this Act.

§ 5. Loyalty

A trustee shall invest and manage the trust assets solely in the interest of the beneficiaries.

§ 6. Impartiality

If a trust has two or more beneficiaries, the trustee shall act impartially in investing and managing the trust assets, taking into account any differing interests of the beneficiaries.

§ 7. Investment Costs.

In investing and managing trust assets, a trustee may only incur costs that are appropriate and reasonable in relation to the assets, the purposes of the trust, and the skills of the trustee.

§ 8. Reviewing Compliance.

Compliance with the prudent investor rule is determined in light of the facts and circumstances existing at the time of a trustee's decision or action and not by hindsight.

§ 9. Delegation of Investment and Management Functions.

(a)   A trustee may delegate investment and management functions that a prudent trustee of comparable skills could properly delegate under the circumstances. The trustee shall exercise reasonable care, skill, and caution in:

(1)   selecting an agent;

(2)   establishing the scope and terms of the delegation, consistent with the purposes and terms of the trust; and

(3)   periodically reviewing the agent's actions in order to monitor the agent's performance and compliance with the terms of the delegation.

(b)   In performing a delegated function, an agent owes a duty to the trust to exercise reasonable care to comply with the terms of the delegation.

(c)   A trustee who complies with the requirements of subsection (a) is not liable to the beneficiaries or to the trust for the decisions or actions of the agent to whom the function was delegated.

(d)   By accepting the delegation of a trust function from the trustee of a trust that is subject to the law of this state, an agent submits to the jurisdiction of the courts of this state.

§ 10.   Language Invoking Standards of Act.

The following terms or comparable language in the provisions of a trust, unless otherwise limited or modified, authorizes any investment or strategy permitted under this Act: "investments permissible by law for investment of trust funds," "legal investments," "authorized investments," "using the judgment and care under the circumstances then prevailing that persons of prudence, discretion, and intelligence exercise in the management of their own affairs, not in regard to speculation but in regard to the permanent disposition of their funds, considering the probable income as well as the probable safety of their capital," "prudent man rule," "prudent trustee rule," and "prudent investor rule."

§ 11.   Application to Existing Trusts.

This Act applies to trusts existing on and created after its effective date. As applied to trusts existing on its effective date, this Act governs only decisions or actions occurring after that date.

§ 12.   Uniformity of Application and Construction.

This Act shall be applied and construed to effectuate its general purpose to make uniform the law with respect to the subject of this Act among the states enacting it.

§ 13.   Short Title.

This Act may be cited as the "[Name of Enacting State] Uniform Prudent Investor Act."

§ 14.   Severability.

§ 15.   Effective Date.

This Act takes effect _____.

§ 16.   Repeals.

The following acts and parts of acts are repealed:

The purpose of the UPIA is to bring the standard of care expected of a trustee up to the standards of the investment management industry as a whole and to codify the new standards of prudence by which the conduct of fiduciaries will be measured. The main reforms embodied in the UPIA are designed to capture for trust beneficiaries the efficiencies and enhanced returns that have been made possible by MPT and resultant investment management practices.

The UPIA makes the following five fundamental changes in the text, scope, and direction of most state trust investment statutes:

(1)   The standard of prudence applies to the trust portfolio as a whole rather than to each individual investment on its own.

(2)   There is a trade-off between risk and return, and a portfolio that is appropriate for one person or trust is not necessarily appropriate for another person or trust.

(3)   Diversification is inherent in prudent investment.

(4)   All specific restrictions on investment types are eliminated; a trustee may invest in anything that plays an appropriate role in achieving risk and return objectives of the trust and that meets the requirements of prudent investing.

(5)   Delegation by a trustee is permissible, subject to certain safeguards.

The UPIA is model uniform legislation and is directly applicable only to trustees in states that have adopted the UPIA. Nevertheless, courts in the future may consider the UPIA the standard governing trust investments. And, although the UPIA does not apply to ERISA fiduciaries or charitable trusts, courts may one day consider it the investment standard for them as well.

The UPIA also recognizes one of the basic principles of trust law, which is that trust law is default law. It provides that the PIR may be expanded, restricted, eliminated, or otherwise altered by the provisions of the trust. Compliance with the PIR and the UPIA is determined in light of the circumstances at the time of the trustee's action, not by hindsight. A trustee is not an insurer or guarantor.

Section 2, which is the heart of the act, defines the standard of care imposed on trustees and includes integral features of that standard such as the employment of portfolio strategy and analysis of risk and return objectives. This section provides an explanatory, but not exhaustive, "laundry list" that a trustee should consider when determining how to manage and invest trust assets. A trustee need not review every item for every account, but only those relevant to the trust or its beneficiaries. This section also includes three provisions on investment policy requiring trustees to

(1)   Make reasonable efforts to verify relevant facts,

(2)   Invest in any kind of property or investment consistent with the standards of the act, and

(3)   Use the special skills or expertise they have represented themselves as possessing.

A trustee must identify the point on the risk and return curve that is appropriate for a specific trust, based on its size, objectives, and beneficiaries. Once the risk and return balance has been identified, portfolio characteristics can be designed to generate the greatest return for the identified level of risk. After asset allocation decisions are made, actual investments are made that meet the risk and return characteristics identified in the portfolio plan. Each of the selected investments must be viewed for its suitability within the trust portfolio and the targeted risk and return characteristics.

If the trustee has developed a trust's investment policy in a manner that reflects the needs and objectives of the trust and its beneficiaries and adheres to the investment policy in a prudent manner, it is reasonable to conclude that courts will view the trustee as having met the UPIA standard of care. The subsequent performance of any investment, or the portfolio in general, should only reflect on the trustee's performance of his duty to monitor the investments, not on his duty to initially develop and invest the trust portfolio.

Like the PIR, the UPIA shifts the legal focus from the performance of an individual security in a portfolio to the portfolio as a whole. The standard of prudence is judged on whether the trustee followed appropriate procedures or processes for managing risk, diversifying assets, and balancing the financial needs of the beneficiaries. Neither the performance of an individual investment nor the overall performance of the portfolio is central to a legal determination of prudence. Prudence is demonstrated by the quality of risk management processes used to develop, implement, and monitor trust investment strategies.

There are no categorical inclusions or exclusions under the UPIA. In other words, no investment is prudent or imprudent per se. Without categoric restrictions on permissible trust investments, specific investments will not be automatically excluded from a particular trust portfolio. The prudence standard recognizes, however, that certain investments may be inappropriate for a particular trust portfolio because of their effect on the risk and return analysis for the trust.

The UPIA emphasizes the importance of diversification in a trust portfolio. A trustee should diversify a trust's investments unless, owing to special circumstances, he or she reasonably determines that the purposes of the trust are better served without diversification. There is no automatic rule or method for identifying how much diversification is enough. This provision creates a statutory presumption that diversification is required and places the burden on trustees to show why trust investments have not been diversified.

The trustee of a new trust, of an old trust to which assets are being added, or of a successor trust should conduct a review of trust assets within a reasonable period of time and decide whether to retain or dispose of those assets. This duty is old trust law and extends to investments that were suitable when acquired but subsequently become unsuitable. This provision derives from the Restatement's admonition that a trustee must constantly monitor a trust's investments. A specific rule for determining a reasonable time is not given, but the criteria and circumstances identified in section 2 as bearing on the prudence of decisions to invest and manage assets also pertain to the prudence of performing reviews of trust assets.

The duty of loyalty expressed in section 5 is perhaps the most characteristic rule of trust law. It requires the trustee to act exclusively for the beneficiaries as opposed to acting for the trustee's own interest or that of third parties. A fiduciary cannot be prudent in the conduct of investment functions if the fiduciary is sacrificing the interests of the beneficiaries. Similarly, section 6 requires a trustee to act impartially when investing and managing trusts assets for two or more beneficiaries. When the trustee owes duties to more than one beneficiary, loyalty requires the trustee to respect the interests of all beneficiaries, especially the conflicts between the interests of income and principal. The UPIA prescribes no regime for allocating receipts of income and principal and the commentary to the UPIA refers to the Revised Uniform Principal and Income Act of 1997.

Section 7 provides that a trustee may incur only costs that are appropriate and reasonable. Wasting beneficiaries' money is imprudent. In devising and implementing investment strategies, trustees are obligated to minimize costs. Trustees should make comparisons on transaction and agent costs such as brokerage commissions, and calculate the cost-benefit ratio, considering the trust's size and ability to bear such costs. These costs include the trustee's own compensation. Although the trustee has a duty to control costs, a trustee is not obligated to pay only the lowest costs.

Consistent with both PIR and ERISA fiduciary standards, the UPIA provides that a trustee may delegate investment management functions that a prudent trustee of comparable skill could properly delegate under the circumstances. A trustee must, however, act prudently in selecting the agent, establishing the scope and terms of the delegation, and periodically reviewing the agent's actions. An agent who accepts delegation by a trustee is subject to jurisdiction of the courts of the state in which the trust is resident.

A trustee who complies with the delegation standards will not be liable to the beneficiaries or to the trust for the agent's decisions or actions. Not every state has adopted this provision, however. The agent is directly liable to the trust and its beneficiaries for the agent's performance pursuant to the delegation. A trustee would be liable to the trust or its beneficiaries for an agent's actions only if the trustee did not prudently make the initial delegation, or did not appropriately and continually monitor the agent's performance. The trustee could also be liable for failing to enforce the terms of the delegation against the agent.

By permitting delegation of a trust's investment and management functions, the UPIA facilitates the outsourcing of functions, such as administration, investment management, tax compliance, and accounting, similar to the outsourcing functions by pension trusts under ERISA. It enhances risk management by permitting trustees to delegate trust investment functions to other investment advisers who have specialized expertise.

Because the trustee is obligated under the UPIA to exercise care, skill, and caution in establishing the terms of a delegation, delegations must not be overly broad. For instance, the commentary to the UPIA states that a prudent delegation by a trustee could not include an exculpation clause protecting an agent from liability for reckless management of trust assets. Leaving the trust beneficiaries without recourse against an agent for the agent's willful wrongdoing would be a breach of the trustee's duty to exercise care, skill, and caution in creating the delegation.

The UPIA provides that it will apply to trusts in existence on the date it is enacted by an adopting state and to trusts created thereafter. As to existing trusts, it applies only to investment decisions and actions made after its effective date.

Appendix C: ERISA Investment Standards

This section provides an overview of the Employment Retirement Income Security Act of 1974 (ERISA) fiduciary investment standards. Bank management should consult with qualified legal counsel to determine whether ERISA's fiduciary investment standards apply to the bank's accounts and, if so, how.

ERISA was a milestone in PIR's evolution. ERISA, which governs fiduciary administration of private employee benefit plans, was the first legislation to adopt elements of MPT as a standard for fiduciary investment conduct and the portfolio-as-a-whole approach to evaluating the prudence of fiduciary investment decisions. Under ERISA, each fiduciary of a plan is required to act with

> the care, skill, prudence, and diligence under the circumstances then prevailing that a prudent person acting in a like capacity and familiar with such matters would use in conducting an enterprise of like character and with like aims.

ERISA was drafted to address Congressional concerns with how private pension plans were funded and with whether the fiduciary duties imposed on persons administering these plans were adequate and consistent. Congress used ERISA's statutory preemption of all conflicting state laws to establish a national standard of fiduciary responsibility for persons administering any aspect of a pension plan. This accomplished Congress' primary goal of protecting pension plan participants in a federal law that subjects plan fiduciaries to a uniform standard, without reference to varying state laws on fiduciary responsibility. It also creates a standard incorporating a liberal and flexible interpretation of the PPR by which a fiduciary's conduct can be measured.

ERISA fiduciaries are subject to the same fundamental duties of loyalty, prudence, and investment diversification as other trustees. Unlike other trustees, ERISA fiduciaries cannot rely on exculpatory language in a fiduciary agreement to relieve them of any of ERISA's prudence requirements. Such language is forbidden by section 410(a) in agreements governing employee benefit plans.

ERISA casts a wide net of fiduciary responsibility. ERISA defines "fiduciary" in terms of functions performed rather than job titles (see section 3(21)(A)). A fiduciary is any person or entity that exercises any discretionary authority or control over the management of the plan or its assets, renders direct or indirect investment advice with respect to plan assets for compensation, has authority or responsibility to render investment advice, or has any discretionary authority or responsibility in the administration of the plan.

An ERISA fiduciary is generally subject to a higher standard of care than a common law trust fiduciary, because ERISA requires a plan fiduciary to act as one who is familiar with such matters. This heightened standard of care has been referred to by some commentators as the ERISA "prudent expert" rule (see section 404(a)(1) and 29 CFR 2550.404a-1). The statutory language has been interpreted by the courts as imposing a relational, flexible standard that requires fiduciaries to act like other trustees in similar circumstances. A plan fiduciary administering a small employee benefit plan will be compared with a trustee administering a small trust, while a plan managing a large pension trust will be compared with a trustee managing a similar trust.

ERISA, its implementing regulations, and court decisions interpreting ERISA generally establish the following:

- The elements of modern portfolio theory have been incorporated into the standard of care governing fiduciaries of employee benefit plans.

- ERISA explicitly prescribes a duty to diversify plan assets to minimize the risk of large losses.

- No investment is labeled prudent or imprudent per se; the universe of investments under ERISA is unlimited.

- Prudence is a rule of conduct rather than performance, and plan fiduciaries should document their decision-making processes concerning the design, implementation, and monitoring of an investment strategy for pension plan assets.

- ERISA allows delegation by permitting a plan to give its fiduciaries authority to delegate investment management functions.

ERISA's recognition of MPT as a significant element in judging fiduciary prudence was clearly emphasized by regulations interpreting the investment

---

duties of plan fiduciaries under ERISA, as promulgated in 1979 by the Department of Labor in 29 CFR 2550.404.a-1. Under this regulatory guidance, a fiduciary charged with investing plan assets will satisfy ERISA obligations "if the fiduciary . . . has given appropriate consideration to those facts and circumstances that . . . the fiduciary knows or should know are relevant to the particular investment or investment course of action involved, including the role the investment or investment course of action plays in the plan's investment portfolio . . . and has acted accordingly."

Appropriate consideration includes, but is not limited to, a determination that the particular course of action is reasonably designed, as part of the portfolio, to further the purposes of the plan, taking into consideration the risk of loss and the opportunity for gain (or other return) associated with the investment or investment course of action. The fiduciary is obligated to consider the composition of the portfolio with regard to diversification, the liquidity and current return of the portfolio relative to anticipated cash flow requirements of the plan, and the projected return of the portfolio relative to the funding objectives of the plan.

ERISA also explicitly prescribes a duty to diversify plan assets to minimize the risk of large losses as a responsibility imposed on a plan fiduciary. However, an ERISA plan fiduciary is relieved of this duty to diversify if it is clearly prudent not to do so under the circumstances (see section 404(a)(1)(C)). Congress directed plan fiduciaries making diversification decisions to consider the following:

- The purpose of the plan;

- The amount of plan assets;

- General financial and industrial conditions;

- The type of investment, whether mortgages, bonds, shares of stock, or otherwise;

- Distribution across geographical locations;

- Distribution across industries; and

- Dates of maturity.

ERISA does not label any investment as prudent or imprudent per se. The result is virtually no restriction on the universe of available investment opportunities. Thus, while the particular selection of investments from that universe could be imprudent, the universe itself is unrestricted. Prudent investing under ERISA should be documented by a systematic and procedural analysis of the proposed investment and its function within the plan's investment portfolio overall.

Plan fiduciaries are not expected to be infallible, and hindsight is not a viable method for assessing whether a fiduciary's investment decisions were prudent at the time the investment was made. Courts have based findings of imprudence largely on a fiduciary's failure to undertake a careful, independent inquiry into the merits of the investment. Emphasis has been placed on the competency of the fiduciary in executing his or her duties and the process followed in evaluating the suitability of an investment in the context of the entire portfolio.

ERISA permits a pension plan to authorize its fiduciaries to appoint an investment manager or managers to acquire, manage, and dispose of the plan's assets (see section 404(c)(3)). ERISA expressly relieves trustees of the exclusive responsibility for managing and controlling plan assets when the authority to manage, acquire, or dispose of those assets has been properly delegated to a qualified investment manager. A qualified investment manager is

- A bank,
- An investment manager registered with the SEC under the Investment Advisors Act of 1940, or
- An insurance company which is qualified under the laws of more than one state to perform services.

The investment manager must acknowledge in writing its fiduciary status with the plan. Named fiduciaries, including trustees, are not responsible for the actions of the investment manager if

- The investment manager was prudently chosen and retained;
- The investment manager does not violate the fiduciary responsibilities of section 404(a)(1); and
- The named fiduciary appropriately monitors the performance of the investment manager.

Although ERISA directly applies only to fiduciaries administering private employee benefit funds, it is an important source of law for the regulation of other fiduciaries. Since a large percentage of the common stock of American companies is owned by pension funds, the conduct of those pension fund fiduciaries and the standards by which their conduct is evaluated is instructive in determining whether a corporate fiduciary acted prudently in investing personal trust assets in common stock. ERISA has had a significant influence on efforts to define "prudence" for all fiduciaries.

Appendix D: Investment Management and 12 CFR 9

National banks serving in a fiduciary capacity must comply with 12 CFR 9, Fiduciary Activities of National Banks. The following discussion covers selected sections of the regulation that relate to investment management.

12 CFR 9.4(a), Administration

The authority to administer and manage discretionary assets in fiduciary accounts may be assigned by the board of directors. The responsibility, however, for proper supervision of fiduciary assets remains with the board. A board must ensure that it is receiving adequate and timely reports to effectively assess and monitor risks in this line of business.

12 CFR 9.4(c), Administration

A national bank may enter into an agency agreement with another entity to purchase or sell services related to the exercise of fiduciary powers. In the context of investment management, this section authorizes a national bank to delegate its fiduciary authority to third-party service providers such as investment managers, advisers, property managers, appraisers, and custodians. When a national bank does delegate its investment authority, it should have the written contract reviewed by counsel to ensure that the contract complies with applicable law. If applicable, the PIR requires a fiduciary to exercise reasonable care, skill, and caution when selecting an agent and establishing the scope and terms of the delegation. It requires the fiduciary to monitor the agent's performance and compliance with the contract.

12 CFR 9.5, Policies and procedures

A national bank engaged in this activity must adopt and follow written policies and procedures for fiduciary investment management services. When appropriate, these policies and procedures should specifically address brokerage placement services, the use of material inside information, self-dealing and conflicts of interest, the selection and retention of legal counsel, and funds awaiting investment or distribution. Policies and procedures must be adequate to ensure compliance with applicable law.

12 CFR 9.6, Review of fiduciary accounts

This section describes three types of reviews for fiduciary accounts:

- Pre-acceptance,
- Initial post-acceptance, and
- Annual reviews.

The first type of review may be the most important to the bank because it represents the initial risk assessment and decision-making event for a specific account. The bank must review the proposed account to determine whether it can properly administer the account. The board, or its designee, should adopt policies that reflect the bank's administrative capabilities and define criteria for accepting or declining new business. This review is applicable to all fiduciary accounts.

When a bank accepts an account, it must promptly review all of the account's discretionary assets to determine if they are appropriate for the account. The regulation does not specifically define the term "promptly," so this time frame is left to the bank's discretion consistent with applicable fiduciary law standards. Only accounts in which the bank has investment discretion must be reviewed. In the context of the portfolio management processes described in appendix A, the initial post-acceptance review is a part of developing the portfolio's investment policy.

Every calendar year thereafter, the person or committee in charge of an account's investments determines whether the current investments are appropriate individually and collectively, given the objectives, risk tolerance, and other constraints of the account. This review is only applicable to discretionary fiduciary accounts. When conducting annual reviews, a bank should look first to any investment provisions in the governing instrument, then to the investment standards found in relevant statutes and case law; the bank should conduct its reviews according to these provisions and standards. Annual reviews required by the regulation can be part of the portfolio monitoring processes described in appendix A.

Account reviews do not have to be written, but the bank must be able to demonstrate that all required reviews have been performed. If a bank adopts a review system in which reviews are not documented individually, the bank must be able to demonstrate that its review system is designed to perform all required reviews and that the reviews are completed.

12 CFR 9.10, Fiduciary funds awaiting investment or distribution

Funds in discretionary fiduciary accounts must be invested or distributed in a reasonable time frame and consistent with applicable law. The bank must also obtain a rate of return for such funds that is consistent with applicable law. A bank can deposit fiduciary account funds awaiting investment or distribution in the bank's deposit accounts unless prohibited by applicable law. The bank must set aside acceptable collateral as security for funds not insured by the Federal Deposit Insurance Corporation. Collateral market value must at all times equal or exceed the amount of the uninsured funds.

12 CFR 9.11, Investment of fiduciary funds

National banks must invest fiduciary account funds in accordance with applicable law. The general order of applicable law is the governing instrument, state and federal law, court orders, and common fiduciary law standards. In most states, national banks will generally be held to the prudent investor standards of a professional investment portfolio manager or adviser. Banks should be guided by general industry standards for investment management and advisory services.

12 CFR 9.12, Self-dealing and conflicts of interest

The section specifies certain investments, loans, and asset sales practices involving discretionary fiduciary accounts that are not permitted unless authorized by applicable law. Applicable law includes the governing instrument, state and federal law, court orders, and common law fiduciary standards. These restrictions are fully discussed in the "Conflicts of Interest" booklet of the *Comptroller's Handbook*.

It should be recognized that authorization by applicable law does not automatically make any particular transaction appropriate or prudent. The fiduciary must still ensure and document that such discretionary transactions are prudent and in the beneficiaries' best interest.

12 CFR 9.18, Collective investment funds

This section provides guidelines for the establishment and administration of collective investment funds by national banks. Please refer to the *Comptroller's Handbook for Fiduciary Activities* for information on collective investment funds.

Appendix E: Investment Policy Statements

An investment policy statement (IPS) is a written document that establishes a portfolio's investment objectives and strategies for a specified period of time. The policy may include investment constraints such as liquidity needs, tax considerations, regulatory requirements, and special circumstances of the client. A properly developed policy supports long-term investment discipline and helps prevent ad-hoc revisions of strategy prompted by panic or overconfidence. An investment policy is an effective risk management tool provided it is understood, agreed with, and consistently followed.

Investment Policy Benefits

Documentation and support for investment decisions: The IPS can be critical evidence in the defense against litigation or accusations of imprudence and disloyalty. It can also provide valuable documentation in support of fiduciary competence and prudence during probate or estate proceedings. Failure to create such a formal statement invites a presumption of imprudent conduct.

Continuity of strategy: As a source document, the IPS provides continuity when changes occur in trustees, portfolio managers, and board or committee members. It minimizes second-guessing and questions about decisions over time, and it reduces a strategy's vulnerability to subsequent review questions.

Investor confidence: The IPS is a tangible document that adds discipline and substance to the investment management process. It gives the client confidence that his or her money is being invested appropriately. It also helps the client to understand the investment process and what to expect from the portfolio manager.

Calming effect during adverse market conditions: The IPS provides assurance and comfort during difficult market conditions. It reminds managers and clients of the purpose of the investment objectives and strategies and the risks inherent in the portfolio.

Baseline to monitor portfolio performance: The IPS establishes goals, objectives, and appropriate performance benchmarks for the portfolio. Using them, the fiduciary manager and client can evaluate the portfolio manager's performance. It establishes the framework against which proposed strategy changes may be evaluated.

Structure and Content

The IPS combines elements of planning and philosophy, and, although not legally required, it clearly establishes investment intent. The primary fiduciary manager, in close consultation with the client, should develop the IPS. It should be formalized, clearly written, and agreed to by all parties involved. The IPS may be structured along the following lines:

Portfolio Background and Purpose

This section explains the reasons for establishing the IPS and the portfolio's purpose, legal structure, size, and tax status. It may describe the portfolio's relationship to other assets the client may own and the likelihood and amount of future contributions to and distributions from the portfolio. For employee benefit plans, a description of the financial health of the sponsor and participant demographics may be appropriate.

Statement of Objectives and Constraints

This section declares portfolio goals and return requirements subject to the risk tolerance and constraints imposed by the client and applicable law. Objectives should be depicted in terms of return requirements, risk tolerance, and other constraints such as time horizon, liquidity, taxes, legal and regulatory issues, and unique needs and circumstances. Return requirements should be specific to the needs and objectives of the account and should not be merely oblique references to such general requirements as "income" and/or "capital growth."

Investment Policy /Strategic Asset Allocation Guidelines

Investment policy guidelines outline the investment strategy and asset allocation plan. The guidelines should be specific enough to establish the desired investment management framework, yet allow enough latitude for reasonable flexibility on the part of investment managers. They must be consistent with the objectives, risk tolerance, and constraints of the client. They should be written with clarity and simplicity so a third-party reviewer can fully understand them.

This section can include strategic asset allocation and re-balancing guidelines. Strategic asset allocation establishes what percentage of the portfolio each asset category should comprise over the investment time frame. Percentage ranges are often used for each category. When an asset category position differs from the percentage, or range of percentage, established for that category, re-balancing may be necessary. Re-balancing is buying or selling investments to make allocations conform to their limits. Re-balancing guidelines, which define when an asset category should be adjusted, are necessary to maintain a policy's consistency and a portfolio manager's discipline.

Investment Guidelines

This section defines the types of investments within each asset category that are appropriate for the client's portfolio. Guidelines may detail authorized portfolio exposures to security instruments, economic sectors, countries, cash holdings, quality, etc.

Selection of Investment Managers/Advisers

An IPS should state how third-party investment managers and advisers are selected and monitored, if applicable. The approach should be systematic and documented. The key is to obtain enough information to ensure that the selected manager has the ability and commitment to strictly adhere to the IPS and applicable law. Refer to appendix F, "Guidelines for Selecting Investment Managers and Advisers," for additional information.

Control and Monitoring Processes

If appropriate for the client, the IPS establishes guidelines for monitoring investment performance, compliance with applicable law, economic trends, and capital markets. The IPS should establish the timing and content of information reports, the parties responsible for completing the reviews, and the documentation standards for monitoring activities. The specific duties and requirements of service providers should be described in the IPS.

The IPS can establish and reference specific performance measurement criteria and benchmarks for the portfolio and its individual asset categories. The guidelines can include a discussion of items that trigger an immediate review of the portfolio such as changes in managers, account principals, beneficiaries, and ownership. Losses of a certain size may also bring a review. Guidance may also define the type and level of portfolio performance that would trigger a bank to review whether it is prudent to continue using a certain manager.

Investment Policy Problems

An investment policy is weak if it:

- Lacks specificity.

- Fails to establish appropriate and realistic goals and objectives.

A fiduciary investment management organization is weak if it fails to:

- Effectively monitor client circumstances, economic trends, and capital markets, updating investment policies as conditions warrant.

- Ensure that portfolio managers consistently apply investment policy guidelines, preventing them from making ad hoc changes based on short-term views.

- Effectively monitor compliance with the bank's investment management policies and applicable law.

Investment Policy Statement Sample Format

I. Account/Client Type and Identification

II. Account Purpose and Background

General statement of purpose and background of client and portfolio.

III. Portfolio Objectives and Constraints

Return Expectations

- Level sought
- Composition: income, capital gains, currency appreciation
- Risk-adjusted: market, inflation, currency

Risk Tolerance

- High, medium, low.
- Specific comments on the risk tolerance characteristics of the client/beneficiaries.
- Reference to specific individual risk factors such as market, interest rate, currency, country, industry, etc.

Constraints

- Time horizon.
- Liquidity.
- Taxes.
- Regulation.
- Legal issues.
- Unique needs and circumstances.

    - Trust beneficiaries.
    - Investment restrictions.
    - Social/political concerns.

IV. Investment Policy Guidelines

- Strategic asset allocation.

- Re-balancing.
- Income distribution.

V.   Investment Guidelines

- Equity (public and private).
- Fixed income (public and private).
- Real estate (public and private).
- Derivatives.
- Mutual funds.
- Hedge funds.
- Mineral interests.
- Timber.
- Other (art, collectibles, precious metals).

VI.   Investment Manager/Adviser Selection Guidelines

VII.   Risk Monitoring and Performance Measurement Guidelines

- Types of reporting mechanisms, documentation standards, and the parties responsible.
- Performance benchmarks and measurement standards.
- Frequency.
- Ticklers for tracking information.

Summary

An investment policy statement may be the most important document a fiduciary manager prepares for an account. Rather than a static or historical document, it is a dynamic instrument for the fiduciary and client to use. The document should ensure frequent communication with a client, prudent investment guidelines, and thorough monitoring and documentation.

Appendix F: Guidelines for Selecting Investment Managers and Advisers

Decisions concerning the delegation of investment authority to a third party are matters of fiduciary judgement and discretion and require the exercise of care, skill, and caution. At a minimum, a fiduciary manager should obtain full information on an investment firm's investment and business approaches, professional resources, financial strength, historical performance, regulatory history, personnel turnover, comparative fees, and other relevant factors.

Fiduciary managers should review the following items when considering investment firms for providing investment management and advisory services to the bank. The information is presented merely to assist in the selection process and does not supersede any provisions of applicable law.

Firm Background

- Name, date established, ownership, affiliations.
- Description of investment products and strategies.
- Past judgments against the firm or its employees, current litigation, and regulatory actions.
- Amount of fully discretionary assets under management, trends.
- Number of taxable accounts and percent of total accounts that are taxable.
- Copies of recent financial audits, if available.

Investment Methodology

- Description and inception date of investment philosophy and strategies.
- Description of investment styles used.

    - How are securities selected? How is a client assured of obtaining the best execution on security trades?
    - Who makes investment decisions?
    - Where is research developed (internally or externally)?
    - What types of valuation models are used and how are they tested?
    - Describe soft dollar arrangements with brokers, if applicable.

- Description of strategies for taxable clients.

- Describe how the firm adapts its strategy to the circumstances of taxable clients.
- Is there access to tax-lot accounting information?
- Can the firm amortize or accrete fixed income securities?
- What is the firm's normal portfolio turnover? How are portfolios monitored for consistency with client needs and circumstances?

Risk Management Processes

- Copies of policies and procedures.
- Description of insurance coverage.
- Describe diversification guidelines or concentration limits for the following factors:

  - Countries/currencies.
  - Industry sectors.
  - Issuers.
  - Securities.
  - Capitalization.
  - P/E, price-to-book ratios.
  - Leverage (portfolio borrowing and derivative usage).

- Methods of monitoring fixed income quality, duration, return, and distribution.
- Risk measurement and reporting systems.
- Internal compliance and audit programs.
- Contingency planning and disaster control systems

Management/Personnel

- Provide biographical sketches of senior firm managers.
- Provide names and experience of investment managers in firm by investment product and style.
- Provide names and experience of traders, analysts, or others with significant responsibilities in the firm.
- Provide the name and role of third-party service providers.

Investment Performance

- Provide short- and long-term investment performance reports for applicable styles, portfolios, and other investment products.
- Does the firm comply with the Association for Investment Management and Research (AIMR) performance presentation standards? Provide such a presentation, if available, including dispersion information.
- Are performance results audited? At what level of AIMR verification?
- How does the firm price securities and positions?
- Explain the firm's processes for developing benchmarks and assessing performance against established benchmarks.

Compensation/Fees

- Provide fee schedules. Will the firm negotiate fees?
- Does the firm manage separate accounts? If so, what is the minimum size?
- Will the firm aggregate assets when calculating fees for accounts related to a single family?
- Does the firm have a hurdle or high watermark for incentive fees?
- Is there a lock-up period?
- How early does a withdrawal notice have to be received?
- Has the firm ever exercised the option to forbid investors from withdrawing from a fund?

Reporting Capabilities

- Sample a client report, a Form ADV, an offering memorandum, a subscription document, and a schedule K-1 for the product or strategy.
- Describe client reporting capability and time frames.
- Are prices and positions reconciled with custodians?
- What type of market and portfolio commentary does the firm provide to clients and consultants, and how quickly does the firm provide it after the end of a period?
- Can the firm provide an after-tax return spreadsheet similar to the one in the AIMR proposal?

In general, the fiduciary manager should obtain as much information as possible. Problems arise not when a fiduciary has done too much, but when it has done too little. If necessary, seek advice and recommendations from other experts and consultants in the field. Consider and interview several firms before making the final decision. The due diligence process should be thoroughly documented and reviewed by appropriate risk managers prior to the execution of a contract with a third party.

Appendix G: Investment Management Policy Guidelines

Investment policies should establish a framework that enables the board and senior management to form business strategies and risk management processes that are consistent with the bank's risk tolerance and financial goals and objectives. In accordance with 12 CFR 9.5, Fiduciary Activities of National Banks, Policies and Procedures, a national bank administering fiduciary accounts must adopt and follow written policies and procedures that are adequate to ensure compliance with applicable law.

This appendix presents an organizational framework for establishing an appropriate policy for investment management services. It is not intended to be all-inclusive, but merely a guide that banks may use for structure and general content. A national bank must make its own determination of policy organization and content based on its diversity and complexity of operation.

Investment Philosophy and Culture

- Organization's statement of philosophy or purpose.
- Fiduciary duties and responsibilities.
- Investment styles.
- Risk tolerance.
- Code of ethics/employee conduct.
- Conflicts of interests.

Products and Services

- Types and size of managed or advised accounts.
- List and description of investment products or styles offered.
- Compensation schedules.
- Description of marketing and distribution channels.
- Policies and procedures for the development of new products and services.

Organization and Supervision

- Organizational structure.
- Defined lines of authority and responsibility.
- Standards for delegating authority and granting approvals.
- Relationships with affiliated organizations.
- Personnel practices:

  - Qualifications and hiring processes.
  - Compensation policies.
  - Performance evaluation.
  - Training program.
  - Code of conduct/disciplinary policies.
  - Personal trading guidelines and penalties.

Portfolio Management Processes

- Account acceptance and periodic review guidelines.

  - Guidelines for pre-acceptance, initial, and annual reviews and documentation standards.
  - Client disclosures; information guidelines.
  - Adherence to investment objectives and guidelines.
  - Investment performance.
  - Program success and strategic revision.

- Standards for economic and capital market analyses.
- Development and implementation of the investment policy program.

  - Establishing investment objectives.
  - Asset allocation modeling processes/model portfolio construction.
  - Investment selection criteria and risk control limits.

    - ❑ For all asset categories, including financial derivatives; separate policy guidelines for each.
    - ❑ Guidelines for temporarily investing permanent portfolio assets.

- Benchmark selection, creation, and monitoring.
- Investment performance calculation, analytics, attribution, and reporting processes.
- Investment research processes.
- Portfolio trading processes.

  - ❑ Selection of brokers/counterparties.
  - ❑ Best execution.
  - ❑ Soft dollars, commissions, and rebates.
  - ❑ Allocations, churning, and cross trading.

- Use of third-party service providers.

  - Selection criteria.
  - Contract criteria.
  - Monitoring and reporting criteria.

Information Systems

- Management information reports.
- Accounting and other record keeping systems.
- Portfolio management systems.

  - Valuation.
  - Performance analytics and attribution.
  - Risk measurement and reporting.
  - Simulations.
  - Trading interface.

- Trading systems.
- Disaster contingency plans.

Reporting and Monitoring

- Types, frequency, and receiving entity of internal investment performance and risk management reports.
- Policy exception tracking and reporting processes.
- Guidelines for reports to clients.
- Control self-assessment program.
- Stress testing, back testing, and model validation processes.

- Customer complaint resolution procedures.
- Third-party service provider reviews.

Compliance Program

- Program description, responsibility, and accountability.
- Operating procedures.
- Reporting and follow-up.
- Summaries of applicable law.

As of May 17, 2012, this guidance applies to federal savings associations in addition to national banks.*

References

Laws

Employee Retirement Income Security Act of 1974
The Gramm-Leach-Bliley Act of 1999
Investment Advisors Act of 1940
Investment Company Act of 1940
Securities Act of 1933
Securities Exchange Act of 1934

Regulations

12 CFR 9, Fiduciary Activities of National Banks
12 CFR 12, Record Keeping and Confirmation Requirements for
  Securities Transactions
29 CFR 2550.404a-1, ERISA Investment Duties

Treatises

Restatement of the Law, Trusts, 2nd and 3rd, The American Law Institute
Uniform Principal and Income Act of 1997, the National Conference of
  Commissioners on Uniform State Laws
Uniform Prudent Investor Act, the National Conference of
  Commissioners on Uniform State Laws

Comptroller's Handbook

"Asset Management"
"Bank Supervision Process"
"Community Bank Fiduciary Activities Supervision"
"Community Bank Supervision"
"Conflicts of Interest"
"Internal and External Audit"
"Internal Control"
"Large Bank Supervision"

OCC Issuances

OCC Bulletin 98-46, "Uniform Interagency Trust Rating System"

Industry Reference Material

Association for Investment Management and Research
- "Statement of the Standards of Professional Conduct"
- "Performance Presentation Standards"
- "Global Investment Performance Standards"

International Investments, Bruce Solnik, 3rd Edition, 1996.
Investment Analysis and Portfolio Management, Cohen, Zinbarg, and Zeikel,1993.
Investment Analysis and Portfolio Management, Frank K. Reilly, 4th Edition, 1994.
Investments, Bodie, Kane, and Marcus, 2nd Edition, 1993.
The Portfolio Management Process and Its Dynamics, J. Maginn and D. Tuttle, Chapter 1,"Managing Investment Portfolios, A Dynamic Process," 2nd Edition, 1990.

Glossary Websites

www.finance-glossary.com

www.centrex.com/terms.html

www.investorwords.com

www.fp.edu/tools/glossary.asp

www.ingramcontent.com/pod-product-compliance
Lightning Source LLC
Chambersburg PA
CBHW080251290526

45790CB00005B/1772